THE HOUSE OF TORCHY

SEWELL FORD

1st WORLD
LIBRARY
Literary Society

The House of Torchy

Sewell Ford

© 1st World Library, 2007
PO Box 2211
Fairfield, IA 52556
www.1stworldlibrary.com
First Edition

LCCN: 2007934207

Softcover ISBN: 978-1-4218-9678-6
Hardcover ISBN: 978-1-4218-9778-3
eBook ISBN: 978-1-4218-9578-9

Purchase *"The House of Torchy"*
as a traditional bound book at:
www.1stWorldLibrary.com/purchase.asp?ISBN=978-1-4218-9678-6

1st World Library is a literary, educational organization
dedicated to:

- Creating a free internet library of downloadable ebooks

- Hosting writing competitions and offering book publishing
  scholarships.

Interested in more 1st World Library books? contact:
literacy@1stworldlibrary.com
Check us out at: www.1stworldlibrary.com

1ˢᵗ World Library Literary Society

Giving Back to the World

"If you want to work on the core problem, it's early school literacy."

- James Barksdale, former CEO of Netscape

"No skill is more crucial to the future of a child, or to a democratic and prosperous society, than literacy."

- Los Angeles Times

"Literacy... means far more than learning how to read and write... The aim is to transmit... knowledge and promote social participation."

- UNESCO

"Literacy is not a luxury, it is a right and a responsibility. If our world is to meet the challenges of the twenty-first century we must harness the energy and creativity of all our citizens."

- President Bill Clinton

"Parents should be encouraged to read to their children, and teachers should be equipped with all available techniques for teaching literacy, so the varying needs and capacities of individual kids can be taken into account."

- Hugh Mackay

CONTENTS

CHAPTER I

TORCHY AND VEE ON THE WAY

Say, I thought I'd taken a sportin' chance now and then before; but I was only kiddin' myself. Believe me, this gettin' married act is the big plunge. Uh-huh! Specially when it's done offhand and casual, the way we went at it.

My first jolt is handed me early in the mornin' as we piles off the mountain express at this little flag stop up in Vermont, and a roly-poly gent in a horse-blanket ulster and a coonskin cap with a badge on it steps up and greets me cheerful.

"Ottasumpsit Inn?" says he.

"Why, I expect so," says I, "if that's the way you call it. Otto—Otta—Yep, that listens something like it."

You see, Mr. Robert had said it only once, when he handed me the tickets, and I hadn't paid much attention.

"Aye gorry!" says the chirky gent, gatherin' up our hand luggage. "Guess you're the ones we're lookin' for. Got yer trunk-checks handy?"

With that I starts fishin' through my pockets panicky. I finds a railroad folder, our marriage certificate, the keys to the studio apartment I'd hired, the box the ring came in, and—

"Gosh!" says I, sighin' relieved. "Sure I got it."

The driver grins good-natured and stows us into a two-seated sleigh, and off we're whirled, bells jinglin', for half a mile or so through the stinging mornin' air. Next thing I know, I'm bein' towed up to a desk and a hotel register is shoved at me. Just like an old-timer, I dashes off my name—Richard T. Ballard.

The mild-eyed gent with the close-cropped Vandyke and the gold-rimmed glasses glances over at Vee.

"Ah—er—I thought Mrs. Ballard was with you!" says he.

"That's so; she is," says I, grabbin' the pen again and tackin' "Mr. and Mrs." in front of my autograph.

That's why, while we're fixin' up a bit before goin' down to breakfast, I has this little confidential confab with Vee.

"It's no use, Vee," says I. "I'm a rank amateur. We might just as well have rice and confetti all over us. I've made two breaks already, and I'm liable to make more. We can't bluff 'em."

"Who wants to?" says Vee. "I'm not ashamed of being on my honeymoon; are you?"

"Good girl!" says I. "You bet I ain't. I thought the usual line, though, was to pretend you'd—"

"I know," says Vee. "And I always thought that was perfectly silly. Besides, I don't believe we could fool anyone if we tried. It's much simpler not to bother. Let them guess."

"And grin too, eh?" says I. "We'll grin back."

Say, that's the happy hunch. Leaves you with nothing to worry about. All you got to do is go ahead and enjoy yourself, free and frolicsome. So when this imposin' head waitress with the forty-eight bust and the grand duchess air bears down on us majestic, and inquires dignified, "Two, sir?" I don't let it stagger me.

"Two'll be enough," says I. "But whisper. Seein' as we're only startin' in on the twosome breakfast game, maybe you could find something nice and cheerful by a window. Eh?"

It's some breakfast. M-m-m-m! Cute little country sausages, buckwheat cakes that would melt in your mouth, with strained honey to go on 'em.

"Have a fourth buckwheat," says I.

"No fair, keeping count!" says Vee. "I looked the other way when you took your fifth."

Honest, I can't see where we acted much different than we did before. Somehow, we always could find things to giggle over. We sure had a good time takin' our first after-breakfast stroll together down Main Street, Vee in her silver-fox furs and me in my new mink-lined overcoat that Mr. Robert had wished on me casual just before we left.

"Cunnin' little town, eh?" says I. "Looks like a birthday cake."

"Or a Christmas card," says Vee. "Look at this old door with the brass knocker and the green fan-light above. Isn't that

Colonial, though?"

"It's an old-timer, all right," says I. "Hello! Here's a place worth rememberin'—the Woman's Exchange. Now I'll know where to go in case I should want to swap you off."

For which crack I gets shoved into a snowdrift.

It ain't until afternoon that I'm struck with the fact that neither of us knows a soul up here. Course, the landlord nods pleasant to me, and I'd talked to the young room clerk a bit, and the bell-hops had all smiled friendly, specially them I'd fed quarters to. But by then I was feelin' sort of folksy, so I begun takin' notice of the other guests and plannin' who I should get chummy with first.

I drifts over by the fireplace, where two substantial old boys are toastin' their toes and smokin' their cigars.

"Snappy brand of weather they pass out up here, eh?" I throws off, pullin' up a rocker.

They turn, sort of surprised, and give me the once-over deliberate, after which one of them, a gent with juttin' eyebrows, clears his throat and remarks, "Quite bracing, indeed."

Then he hitches around until I'm well out of view, and says to the other:

"As I was observing, an immediate readjustment of international trade balances is inevitable. European bankers are preparing for it. We are not. Only last month one of the Barings cabled—"

I'll admit my next stab at bein' sociable was kind of feeble. In front of the desk is a group of three gents, one of 'em not over fifty or so; but when I edges up close enough to hear what the debate is about, I finds it has something to do with a scheme for revivin' Italian opera in Boston, and I backs off so sudden I almost bumps into a hook-beaked old dame who is waddlin' up to the letter-box.

"Sorry," says I. "I should have honked."

She just glares at me, and if I hadn't side-stepped prompt she might have sunk that parrot bill into my shoulder.

After that I sidles into a corner where I couldn't be hit from behind, and tries to dope out the cause of all this hostility. Did they take me for a German spy or what? Or was this really an old folks' home masqueradin' as a hotel, with Vee and me breakin' in under false pretenses?

So far as I could see, the inmates was friendly enough with each other. The old girls sat around in the office and parlors, chattin' over their knittin' and crochet. The old boys paired off mostly, though some of them only read or played solitaire. A few people went out wrapped up in expensive furs and was loaded into sleighs. The others waved good-by to 'em. But I might have been built out of window-glass. They didn't act as though I was visible.

"Huh!" thinks I. "I'll bet they take notice of Vee when she comes down."

If I'd put anything up on that proposition I'd owed myself money. They couldn't see her any more'n they could me. When we went out for another walk nobody even looked after us. I didn't say anything then, but I kept thinkin'. And all that evenin' we sat around amongst 'em without bein' disturbed.

About eight o'clock an orchestra shows up and cuts loose with music in the ball-room, mostly classic stuff like the "Spring Song" and handfuls plucked from "Aida." We slips in and listens. Then the leader gets his eye on us and turns on a fox-trot.

"Looks like they was waitin' for us to start something," says I. "Let's."

We'd gone around three or four times when Vee balks. About twenty-five old ladies, with a sprinklin' of white-whiskered old codgers, had filed in and was watchin' us solemn and critical from the side-lines. Some was squintin' disapprovin' through their lorgnettes, and I noticed a few whisperin' to each other. Vee quits right in the middle of a reverse.

"Do they think we are giving an exhibition?" she pouts.

"Maybe we're breakin' some of the rules and by-laws," says I. "Anyway, I think we ought to beat it before they call in the high sheriff."

Next day it was just the same. We was out part of the time, indulgin' in walks and sleigh rides; but nobody seemed to see us, goin' or comin'. And I begun to get good and sore.

"Nice place, this," says I to Vee, as we trails in to dinner that evenin'. "Almost as sociable as the Grand Central station."

Vee tries to explain that it's always like this in these exclusive little all-the-year-round joints where about the same crowd of people come every season.

"Then you have to be born in the house to be a reg'lar person, I suppose?" says I.

Well, it's about then I notices this classy young couple who are makin' their way across the dinin'-room, bein' hailed right and left. And next thing I know, the young lady gets her eye on Vee, stops to take another look, then rushes over and gives her the fond clinch from behind.

"Why you dear old Verona!" says she.

"Judith!" gasps Vee, kind of smothery.

"Whatever are you doing up—" And then Judith gets wise to me sittin' opposite. "Oh!" says she.

Vee blushes and exhibits her left hand.

"It only happened the other night," says she. "This is Mr. Ballard, Judith. And you?"

"Oh, ages ago—last spring," says Judith. "Bert, come here."

It's a case of old boardin'-school friends who'd lost track of each other. Quite a stunner, young Mrs. Nixon is, too, and Bert is a good match for her. The two girls hold quite a reunion, with us men standin' around lookin' foolish.

"We're living in Springfield, you know," goes on Judith, "where Bert is helping to build another munition plant. Just ran up to spend the week-end with Auntie. You've met her, of course?"

"We—we haven't met anyone," says Vee.

"Why, how funny!" exclaims Mrs. Nixon. "Please come over right now."

"My dear," says Auntie, pattin' Vee chummy on the hand,

"we have all been wondering who you two young people were. I knew you must be nice, but—er—Come, won't you join us at this table? We'll make just a splendid little family party. Now do!"

Oh, yes, we did. And after dinner I'll be hanged if we ain't introduced to almost everybody in the hotel. It's a reg'lar reception, with folks standin' in line to shake hands with us. The old boy with the eye awnin's turns out to be an ex-Secretary of the Treasury; an antique with a patent ear-'phone has been justice of some State Supreme Court; and so on. Oh, lots of class to 'em. But after I'd been vouched for by someone they knew they all gives me the hearty grip, offers me cigars, and hopes I'm enjoyin' my stay.

"And so you are a niece of dear Mrs. Hemmingway?" says old Parrot-Face, when her turn comes. "Think of that! And this is your husband!" And then she says how nice it is that some other young people will be up in the mornin'.

That evenin' Judith gets busy plannin' things to do next day.

"You haven't tried the toboggan chute?" says she. "Why, how absurd!"

Yep, it was a big day, Saturday was. Half a dozen more young folks drifted in, includin' a couple of Harvard men that Vee knew, a girl she'd met abroad, and another she'd seen at a house-party. They was all live wires, too, ready for any sort of fun. And we had all kinds. Maybe we didn't keep that toboggan slide warm. Say, it's some sport, ain't it?

Anyway, our honeymoon was turnin' out a great success. The Nixons concluded to stay over a few days, and three or four of the others found they could too, so we just went on whooping things up.

Next I knew we'd been there a week, and was due to make a jump to Washington for a few days of sight-seein'.

"I'm afraid that will not be half as nice as this has been," says Vee.

"It couldn't," says I. "It's the reg'lar thing to do, though."

"I hate doing the regular thing," says Vee. "Besides, I'm dying to see our little studio apartment and get settled in it. Why not—well, just go home?"

"Vee," says I, "you got more good sense than I have red hair. Let's!"

CHAPTER II

VEE WITH VARIATIONS

"But—but look here, Vee," says I, after I'd got my breath back, "you can't do a thing like that, you know."

"But I have, Torchy," says she; "and, what is more, I mean to keep on doing it."

She don't say it messy, understand—just states it quiet and pleasant.

And there we are, hardly at the end of our first month, with the rocks loomin' ahead.

Say, where did I collect all this bunk about gettin' married, anyway? I had an idea that after the honeymoon was over, you just settled down and lived happy, or otherwise, ever after. But, believe me, there's nothing to it. It ain't all over, not by a long shot. As a matter of fact, you've just begun to live, and you got to learn how.

Here I am, discoverin' a new Vee every day or so, and almost dizzy tryin' to get acquainted with all of 'em. Do I show up that way to her? I doubt it. Now and then, though, I catch her watchin' me sort of puzzled.

So there's nothing steady goin' or settled about us yet, thanks be. Home ain't a place to yawn in. Not ours. We don't get all our excitement out of changin' the furniture round, either. Oh, sure, we do that, too. You know, we're startin' in with a ready-made home—a studio apartment that Mr. Robert picked up for me at a bargain, all furnished.

He was a near-artist, if you remember, this Waddy Crane party, who'd had a bale of coupon-bearin' certificates willed to him, and what was a van-load of furniture more or less to him? Course, I'm no judge of such junk, but Vee seems to think we've got something swell.

"Just look at this noble old davenport, will you!" says she. "Isn't it a beauty? And that highboy! Real old San Domingo mahogany that is, with perfectly lovely crotch veneer in the panels. See?"

"Uh-huh," says I.

"And this four-poster with the pineapple tops and the canopy," she goes on. "Pure Colonial, a hundred years old."

"Eh?" says I, gazin' at it doubtful. "Course, I was lookin' for second-hand stuff, but I don't think he ought to work off anything that ancient on me, do you?"

"Silly!" says Vee. "It's a gem, and the older the better."

"We'll need some new rugs, won't we," says I, "in place of some of these faded things?"

"Faded!" says Vee. "Why, those are Bokharas. I will say for Mr. Crane that he has good taste. This is furnished so much better than most studios—nothing useless, no mixing of periods."

"Oh, when I go out after a home," says I, "I'm some grand little shopper."

"Pooh!" says Vee. "Who couldn't do it the way you did? Why, the place looks as if he'd just taken his hat and walked out. There are even cigars in the humidor. And his easel and paints and brushes! Do you know what I'm going to do, Torchy?"

"Put pink and green stripes around the cigars, I expect," says I.

"Smarty!" says she. "I'm going to paint pictures."

"Why not?" says I. "There's no law against it, and here you got all the tools."

"You know I used to try it a little," says she. "I took quite a lot of lessons."

"Then go to it," says I. "I'll get a yearly rate from a pressing club to keep the spots off me. I'll bet you could do swell pictures."

"I know!" says Vee, clappin' her hands. "I'll begin with a portrait of you. Let me try sketching in your head now."

That's the way Vee generally goes at things—with a rush. Say, she had me sittin' with my chin up and my arms draped in one position until I had a neck-ache that ran clear to my heels.

"Hal-lup!" says I, when both feet was sound asleep and my spine felt ossified. "Couldn't I put on a sub while I drew a long breath?"

At that she lets me off, and after a fifth-innin' stretch I'm called round to pass on the result.

"Hm-m-m!" says I, starin' at what she's done to a perfectly good piece of stretched canvas.

"Well, what does it look like?" demands Vee.

"Why," says I, "I should call it sort of a cross between the Kaiser and Billy Sunday."

"Torchy!" says Vee. "I—I think you're just horrid!"

For a whole week she sticks to it industrious, jottin' down studies of various parts of my map while I'm eatin' breakfast, and workin' over 'em until I come back from the office in the afternoon. Did I throw out any more comic cracks? Never a one—not even when the picture showed that my eyes toed in. All I did was pat her on the back and say she was a wonder. But say, I got so I dreaded to look at the thing.

"You know your hair isn't really red," says Vee; "it—it's such an odd shade."

"Sort of triple pink, eh?" says I.

She squeezes out some more paints, stirs 'em vigorous, and makes another stab. This time she gets a bilious lavender with streaks of fire-box red in it.

"Bother!" says she, chuckin' away the brushes. "What's the use pretending I'm an artist when I'm not? Look at that hideous mess! It's too awful for words. Take away that fire-screen, will you, Torchy?"

And, with the help of a few matches and a sportin' extra, we made quite a cheerful little blaze in the coal grate.

"There!" says Vee, as we watches the bonfire. "So that's over. And it's rather a relief to find out that I haven't got to be a lady artist, after all. What is more, I am positive I couldn't write a book. I'm afraid, Torchy, that I am a most every-day sort of person."

"Maybe," says I, "you're one of the scarce ones that believes in home and hubby."

"We-e-e-ell," says Vee, lockin' her fingers and restin' her chin on 'em thoughtful, "not precisely that type, either. My mind may not be particularly advanced, but the modified harem existence for women doesn't appeal to me. And I must confess that, with kitchenette breakfasts, dinners out, and one maid, I can't get wildly excited over a wholly domestic career. Torchy, I simply must have something to do."

Me, I just sits there gawpin' at her.

"Why," says I, "I thought that when a girl got married she— she—"

"I know," says she. "You think you thought. So did I. But you really didn't think about it at all, and I'm only beginning to. Of course, you have your work. I suppose it's interesting, too. Isn't it?"

"It's a great game," says I. "Specially these days, when doin' any kind of business is about as substantial as jugglin' six china plates while you're balanced on top of two chairs and a kitchen table. Honest, we got deals enough in the air to make you dizzy followin' 'em. If they all go through we'll stand to cut a melon that would pay off the national debt. If they should all go wrong—well, it would be some smash, believe me."

Vee's gray eyes light up sudden.

"Why couldn't you tell me all about some of these deals," she says, "so that I could be in it too? Why couldn't I help?"

"Maybe you could," says I, "if you understood all the fine points."

"Couldn't I learn?" demands Vee.

"Well," says I, "I've been right in the thick of it for quite some years. If you could pick up in a week or so what it's taken me years to—"

"I see," cuts in Vee. "I suppose you're right, too. But I'm sure that I should like to be in business. It must be fascinating, all that planning and scheming. It must make life so interesting."

I nods. "It does," says I.

"Then why shouldn't I try something of the kind, all my very own?" she asks. "Oh, in a small way, at first?"

More gasps from me. This was gettin' serious.

"You don't mean margin dabblin' at one of them parlor bucket-shops, do you?" I demands.

"No fear," says Vee. "I think gambling is just plain stupid. I mean some sort of legitimate business—buying and selling things."

"Oh!" says I. "Like real estate, or imported hats, or somebody's home-made candy? Or maybe you mean startin' one of them Blue Goose novelty shops down in Greenwich Village. I'll tell you. Why not manufacture left-handed collar buttons for the south-paw trade? There's a field."

Vee don't say any more. In fact, three or four days goes by without her mentionin' anything about havin' nothing to do, and I'd 'most forgot this batty talk of ours.

And then, one afternoon when I comes home after a busy day at doin' nothing much and tryin' to look important over it, she greets me with a flyin' tackle and drags me over to a big wingchair by the window.

"What do you think, Torchy?" says she. "I've found something!"

"That trunk key you've been lookin' for?" says I.

"No," says she. "A business opening."

"A slot-machine to sell fudge?" says I.

"You'd never guess," says she.

"Then shoot it," says I.

"I'm going to open a shoe-shinery," she announces.

"Wha-a-a-at!" says I.

"Only I'm not going to call it that," she goes on. "It isn't to be a 'parlor,' either, nor a 'shine shop.' It's to be just a 'Boots.' Right here in the building. I've leased part of the basement. See?" And she waves a paper at me.

"Quit your kiddin'," says I.

But she insists that it's so. Sure enough, that's the way the lease reads.

And that's when, as I was tellin' you, I rises up majestic and announces flat that she simply can't do a thing like that. Also she comes back at me just as prompt by sayin' that she can and will. It's the first time we've met head-on goin' different ways, and I had just sense enough to throw in my emergency before the crash came.

"Now let's get this straight," says I. "I don't suppose you're plannin' to do shoe-shinin' yourself?"

Vee smiles and shakes her head.

"Or 'tend the cash register and sell shoelaces and gum to gentlemen customers?"

"Oh, it's not to be that sort of place," says she. "It's to be an English 'boots,' on a large scale. You know what I mean."

"No," says I.

So she sketches out the enterprise for me. Instead of a reg'lar Tony joint with a row of chairs and a squad of blue-shirted Greeks jabberin' about the war, this is to be a chairless, spittoonless shine factory, where the customer only steps in to sign a monthly contract or register a kick. All the work is to be collected and delivered, same as laundry.

"I would never have thought of it," explains Vee, "if it hadn't been for Tarkins. He's that pasty-faced, sharp-nosed young fellow who's been helping the janitor recently. A cousin, I believe. He's a war wreck, too. Just think, Torchy: he was in the trenches for more than a year, and has only been out of a base hospital two months. They wouldn't let him enlist again; so he came over here to his relatives.

"It was while he was up trying to stop that radiator leak the other day that I asked him if he would take out a pair of my boots and find some place where they could be cleaned. He brought them back inside of half an hour, beautifully done. And when I insisted on being told where he'd taken them, so that I might send them to the same place again, he admitted that he had done the work himself. 'My old job, ma'am,' says he. 'I was boots at the Argyle Club, ma'am, before I went out to strafe the 'Uns. Seven years, ma'am. But they got a girl doin' it now, a flapper. Wouldn't take me back.' Just fancy! And Tarkins a trench hero! So I got to thinking."

"I see," says I. "You're going to set Tarkins up, eh?"

"I'm going to make him my manager," says Vee. "He will have charge of the shop and solicit orders. We are going to start with only two polishers; one for day work, the other for the night shift. And Tarkins will always be on the job. They're installing a 'phone now, and he will sleep on a cot in the back office. We will work this block first, something like four hundred apartments. Later on—well, we'll see."

"I don't want to croak," says I, "but do you think folks will send out their footwear that way? You know, New Yorkers ain't used to gettin' their shines except on the hoof."

"I mean to educate them to my 'boots' system," says Vee. "I'm getting up a circular now. I shall show them how much time they can save, how many tips they can avoid. You see, each customer will have a delivery box, with his name and address on it. No chance for mistakes. The boxes can be set outside the apartment doors. We will have four collections, perhaps; two in the daytime, two at night. And when they see the kind of work we do—Well, you wait."

"I'll admit it don't listen so worse," says I. "The scheme has its good points. But when you come to teachin' New York people new tricks, like sendin' out their shoes, you're goin' to be up against it."

"Then you think I can't make 'boots' pay a profit?" asks Vee.

"That would be my guess," says I. "If it was a question of underwritin' a stock issue for the scheme I'd have to turn it down."

"Good!" says Vee. "Now I shall work all the harder. Tarkins will be around early in the morning to get you as our first customer."

Say, for the next few days she certainly was a busy party—plannin' out her block campaign, lookin' over supply bills, and checkin' up Tarkins's reports.

I don't know when I'd ever seen her so interested in anything, or so chirky. Her cheeks were pink all the time and her eyes dancin'. And somehow we had such a lot to talk about.

Course, though, I didn't expect it to last. You wouldn't look for a girl like Vee, who'd never had any trainin' for that sort of thing, to start a new line and make a go of it right off the bat. But, so long as she wasn't investin' very heavy, it didn't matter.

And then, here last night, after she'd been workin' over her account-books for an hour or so, she comes at me with a whoop, and waves a sheet of paper under my nose excited.

"Now, Mister Business Man," says she, "what do you think of that?"

"Eh?" says I, starin' at the figures.

"One hundred and seventeen regular customers the first week," says she, "and a net profit of $23.45. Now how about underwriting that stock issue?"

Well, it was a case of backin' up. She had it all figured out plain. She'd made good from the start. And, just to prove that it's real money that she's made all by herself, she insists on invitin' me out to a celebration dinner. It's a swell one, too, take it from me.

And afterwards we sits up until long past midnight while Vee plans a chain of "boots" all over the city.

"Gee!" says I. "Maybe you'll be gettin' yourself written up as 'The Shine Queen of New York' or something like that. Lucky Auntie's in Jamaica. Think what a jolt it would give her."

"I don't care," says Vee. "I've found a job."

"Guess you have," says I. "And, as I've remarked once or twice before, you're some girl."

CHAPTER III

A QUALIFYING TURN FOR TORCHY

And here all along I'd been kiddin' myself that I was a perfectly good private sec. Also I had an idea the Corrugated Trust was one of the main piers that kept New York from slumpin' into the North River, and that the boss, Old Hickory Ellins, was sort of a human skyscraper who loomed up as imposin' in the financial foreground as the Metropolitan Tower does on the picture post-cards that ten-day trippers mail to the folks back home.

Not that I'd been workin' up any extra chest measure since I've had an inside desk and had connected with a few shares of our preferred stock; I always did feel more or less that way about our concern. And the closer I got to things, seein' how wide our investments was scattered and how many big deals we stood behind, the surer I was that we was important people.

And then, in trickles this smooth-haired young gent with the broad *a*'s and the full set of *the dansant* manners, to show me where I'm wrong on all counts. He'd succeeded in convincin' Vincent-on-the-gate that nobody around the shop would do but Mr. Ellins himself, so here was Old Hickory standin' in the door of his private office with the card in his hand and starin' puzzled at this immaculate symphony in browns.

"Eh?" says he. "You're from Runyon, are you? Well, I wired him to stop off on his way through and have luncheon with me at the Union League. Know anything about that, do you?"

"Mr. Runyon regrets very much," says the young gent, "that he will be unable to accept your kind invitation. He is on his way to Newport, you know, and—"

"Yes, I understand all that," breaks in Old Hickory. "Daughter's wedding. But that isn't until next week, and while he was in town I thought we might have a little chat and settle a few things."

"Quite so," says the symphony. "Precisely why he sent me up, sir—to talk over anything you might care to discuss."

"With you!" snorts Old Hickory. "Who the brocaded buckboards are you?"

"Mr. Runyon's secretary, sir," says the young gent. "Bixby's the name, sir, as you will see by the card, and—"

"Ha!" growls old Hickory. "So that's Marc Runyon's answer to me, is it? Sends his secretary! Very well; you may talk with *my* secretary. Torchy!"

"Right here!" says I, slidin' to the front.

"Take this person somewhere," says Mr. Ellins, jerkin' his thumb at Bixby; "instruct him what to tell his master about how we regard that terminal hold-up; then dust him off carefully and lead him to the elevator."

"Got you!" says I, salutin'.

You might think that would have jolted Mr. Bixby. But no. He gets the door shut in his face without even blinkin' or gettin' pink under the eyes. Don't even indulge in any shoulder shrugs or other signs of muffled emotion. He just turns to me calm and remarks businesslike:

"At your service, sir."

Now, say, this lubricated diplomacy act ain't my long suit as a general thing, but I couldn't figure a percentage in puttin' over any more rough stuff on Bixby. It rolled off him too easy. Course, it might be all right for Mr. Ellins to get messy or blow a gasket if he wanted to; but I couldn't see that it was gettin' us anywhere. He hadn't planned this luncheon affair just for the sake of being sociable—I knew that much. The big idea was to get next to Marcus T. Runyon and thresh out a certain proposition on a face-to-face basis. And if he chucked that overboard because of a whim, we stood to lose.

It was up to me now, though. Maybe I couldn't be as smooth as this Bixby party, but I could make a stab along that line. It would be good practice, anyhow. So I tows him over to my corner, and arranges him easy in an armchair.

"As between private secs, now," says I, "what's puttin' up the bars on this get-together motion, eh?"

Well, considerin' that Bixby is English and don't understand the American language very well, we got along fine. Once or twice, there, I thought I should have to call in an interpreter; but by bein' careful to state things simple, and by goin' over some of the points two or three times slow, we managed to make out what each other meant.

It seems that Marcus T. is more or less of a frail and tender party. Dashin' out for a Union League luncheon, fillin' himself up on *poulet en casserole* and such truck, not to mention Martinis and demi-tasses and brunette perfectos, was clean out of the question.

"My word!" says Bixby, rollin' his eyes. "His physician would never allow it, you know."

"Suppose he took a chance and didn't tell the doc?" I suggests.

"Impossible," says Bixby. "He is with him constantly—travels with him, you understand."

I didn't get it all at first, but I sopped it up gradual. Marcus T. wasn't takin' any casual flit from his Palm Beach winter home to his Newport summer place. No jumpin' into a common Pullman for him, joinin' the smokin'-room bunch, and scrabblin' for his meals in the diner. Hardly.

He was travelin' in his private car, with his private secretary, his private physician, his trained nurse, his private chef, and most likely, his private bootblack. And he was strictly under his doctor's orders. He wasn't even goin' to have a peek at Broadway or Fifth Avenue; for, although a suite had been engaged for him at the Plutoria, the Doc had ruled against it only that mornin'. No; he had to stay in the private car, that had been run on a special sidin' over in the Pennsylvania yards.

"So you see," says Bixby, spreadin' out his varnished finger-nails helpless. "And yet, I am sure he would very much like to have a chat with his old friend Mr. Ellins."

I had all I could do to choke back a haw-haw. His old friend, eh? Oh, I expect they might be called friends, in a way. They hadn't actually stuck any knives into each other. And 'way back, when they was both operatin' in Chicago, I understand they was together a good deal. But since—Well, maybe at a circus you've seen a couple of old tigers pacin' back and forth in nearby cages and catchin' sight of one another now and then? Something like that.

"Friend" wasn't the way Marcus T. was indexed on our books. If we spotted any suspicious moves in the market, or found one of our subsidiary companies being led astray by unseen hands, or a big contract slippin' away mysterious, the word was always passed to "watch the Runyon interests." And I'll admit that when the Corrugated saw an openin' to put a crimp in a Runyon deal, or overbid 'em on a franchise, or crack a ripe egg on one of their bond issues, we only waited long enough for it to get dark before gettin' busy. Oh, yes, we was real chummy that way.

And then again, with the Runyon system touchin' ours in so many spots, we had a lot of open daylight dealin's. We interlocked here and there; we had joint leases, trackage agreements, and so on, where we was just as trustin' of each other as a couple of gentlemen crooks dividin' the souvenirs after an early mornin' call at a country-house.

This terminal business Old Hickory had mentioned was a sample. Course, I only knew about it in a vague sort of way: something about ore docks up on the Lakes. Anyway, it was a case where the Runyon people had hogged the waterfront and was friskin' us for tonnage charges on every steamer we loaded.

I know it was something that had to be renewed annual, for I'd heard Mr. Ellins beefin' about it more'n once. Last year, I remember, he was worse than usual, which was accounted for later by the fact that the ton rate had been jumped a couple of cents. And now it had been almost doubled. No wonder he wanted a confab with Marcus T. on the subject. And, from where I stood, it looked like he ought to have it, grouch or no grouch.

"Bixby," says I, "Mr. Ellins would just grieve himself sick if this reunion he's planned don't come off. Now, what's the best you can do?"

"If Mr. Ellins could come to the private car—" begins Bixby.

"Say," I breaks in, "you wouldn't ask him to climb over freight-cars and dodge switch-engines just for old times' sake, would you?"

Bixby holds up both hands and registers painful protest.

"By no means," says he. "We would send the limousine for Mr. Ellins, have it wait his convenience, and drive him directly to the car steps. I think I can arrange the interview for any time between two-thirty and four o'clock this afternoon."

"Now, that's talkin'!" says I. "I'll see what I can do with the boss. Wait, will you?"

Oh, boy, though! That was about as tough a job as I ever tackled. Old Hickory still has his neck feathers ruffled, and he's chewin' savage on a black cigar when I go in to slip him the soothin' syrup. First off I explains elaborate what a sick man Mr. Runyon is, and all about the trained nurse and the private physician.

"Bah!" says Old Hickory. "I'll bet he's no more an invalid than I am. Just coddling himself, that's all. Got the private car habit, too! Why, I knew Marc Runyon when he thought an upper berth was the very lap of luxury; knew him when he'd grind his teeth over payin' a ten-dollar fee to a doctor. And now he's trying to buy back his digestion by hiring a private physician, is he? The simple-minded old sinner!"

"I expect you ain't seen much of him lately, Mr. Ellins?" I suggests.

Old Hickory hunches his shoulders careless.

"No," says he.

Then he gazes reminiscent at the ceilin'. I could tell by watchin' his lower jaw sort of loosen up that he was thinkin' of the old days, or something like that. It struck me as a good time to let things simmer. I drops back a step and waits. All of a sudden he turns to me and demands:

"Well, son?"

"If you could get away about three," says I, "Mr. Runyon's limousine will be waiting."

"Huh!" says he. "Well, I'll see. Perhaps."

"Yes, sir," says I. "Then you'll be wanting the dope on that terminal lease. Shall I dig it up?"

"Oh, you might as well," says Old Hickory. "There isn't much, but bring along anything you may find. You will have to serve as my entire retinue, Torchy. I expect you to behave like a regular high-toned secretary."

"Gee!" says I. "That's some order. Mr. Bixby'll have me lookin' like an outside porter. But I'll go wind myself up."

All I could think of, though, was to post myself on that terminal stuff. And, believe me, I waded into that strong. Inside of ten minutes after I'd sent Bixby on his way I had Piddie clawin' through the record safe, two stenographers searchin' the letter-files, and Vincent out buyin' maps of Lake Superior. I had about four hours to use in gettin' wise to the fine points of a deal that had been runnin' on for ten years; but I can absorb a lot of information in a short time when I really get my mind pores open.

At that, though, I expect my head would have been just a junk-heap of back-number facts if I hadn't run across the name of this guy McClave in some of the correspondence. Seems he'd been assistant traffic agent for one of the Runyon lines, but had been dropped durin' a consolidation shake-up. And now he happens to be holdin' down a desk out in our general offices. Just on a chance, I pushes the button for him.

Well, say, talk about tappin' the main feedpipe! Why, that quiet little Scotchman in the shiny black cutaway coat and the baggy plaid trousers, he knew more about how iron ore gets from the mines to the smelters than I do about puttin' on my own clothes. And as for the inside hist'ry of how we got that tonnage charge wished onto us, why, McClave had been called in when the merry little scheme was first plotted out.

I made him start at the beginning and explain every item, while we munched fried-egg sandwiches as we went over reports, sorted out old letters, and marked up a perfectly good map of Minnesota. But by three P.M. I had a leather document case stuffed with papers and a cross-index of 'em in my so-called brain.

"When you're ready, Mr. Ellins," says I, standin' by with my hat in my hand.

"Oh, yes," says he, heavin' himself up reluctant from his desk chair.

And, sure enough, there's a silk-lined limousine and a French chauffeur waitin' in front of the arcade. In no time at all, too, we're rolled across Seventh Avenue, down through a tunnel, and out alongside a shiny private car with a brass-bound bay-window on one end and flower-boxes hung on the side. They even had a carpet laid on the steps. It's a happy little home on wheels.

Also there is Bixby the Busy, with his ear out for us.

Talk about private seccing as a fine art! Why, say, I fairly held my breath watchin' him operate. Every move is as smooth and silent as a steel lathe runnin' in an oil bath. He don't exactly whisper, or give us the hush-up sign, but somehow he gets me steppin' soft and talkin' under my breath from the minute I hits the front vestibule.

"So good of you, Mr. Ellins," he coos soothin'. "Will you come right in? Mr. Runyon will be with you in a moment. Just finishing a treatment, you know. This way, gentlemen."

Say, it was like bein' ushered into church durin' the prayer. Once inside, you'd never guess it was just a car. More like the corner of a perfectly good drawin'-room—easy chairs, Turkish rugs, silver vases full of roses, double hangin's at the windows.

"Will you sit here, Mr. Ellins?" murmurs Bixby. "And you here, sir. Pardon me a moment."

Then he glides about, pullin' down a shade, movin' a vase, studyin' how the light is goin' to strike in, pattin' a cushion, shovin' out a foot-rest—like he was settin' the stage for the big scene. And right in the midst of it I near spilled the beans by pullin' an afternoon edition out of my pocket. Bixby swoops down on me panicky.

"Oh, I'm so sorry!" says he, pluckin' the paper out of my fingers. "But may I put this outside? Mr. Runyon cannot stand the rustling of newspapers. Please don't mind. There! Now I think we are ready."

I wanted to warn him that I hadn't quite stopped breathin' yet, but he's off to the other end of the room, where a nurse in a white cap is peekin' through the draperies.

Bixby nods to her and stands one side. Then we waits a minute—two minutes. And finally the procession appears.

First, a nurse carryin' a steamer rug; next, another nurse with a tray; and after them a valet and the private physician with the great Marcus T. walkin' slow between.

He ain't so imposin' when you get that close, though. Kind of a short, poddy party, who looks like he'd been upholstered generous once but had shrunk a lot. There are heavy bags under his eyes, dewlaps at his mouth-corners, and deep seams across his clean-shaved face. He has sort of a cigar-ash complexion. And yet, under them shaggy brows is a keen pair of eyes that seem to take in everything.

Old Hickory gets up right off, with his hand out. But it's a social error. Bixby blocks him off graceful. He's in full command, Bixby is. With a one-finger gesture he signals the nurse to drape her rug over the chair. Then he nods to the doctor and the valet to go ahead. They ease Runyon into his seat. Bixby motions 'em to wrap up his knees. By an eyelid flutter he shows the other nurse where to set her tray.

It's almost as complicated a process as dockin' an ocean liner. When it's finished, Bixby waves one hand gentle, and they all fade back through the draperies.

"Hello, Ellins," says Runyon. "Mighty good of you to hunt up a wreck like me."

I almost gasped out loud. Somehow, after seem' him handled like a mummy that way, you didn't expect to hear him speak. It's a shock. Even Old Hickory must have felt something as I did.

"I—I didn't know," says he. "When did it happen, Runyon?"

"Oh, it's nothing," says Marcus T. "I am merely paying up for fifty-odd years of hard living by—by this. Ever try to exist on artificial sour milk and medicated hay, Ellins? Hope you never come to it. Don't look as though you would. But you were always tougher than I, even back in the State Street days, eh?"

First thing I knew, they were chattin' away free and easy. Course, there was Bixby all the time, standin' behind watchful. And right in the middle of a sentence he didn't hesitate to butt in and hand Mr. Runyon a glass of what looked like thin whitewash. Marcus T. would take a sip obedient and then go on with his talk. At last he asks if there's anything special he can do for Mr. Ellins.

"Why, yes," says Old Hickory, settin' his jaw. "You might call off your highwaymen on that Manitou terminal lease, Runyon. That is, unless you mean to take all of our mining profits."

Marcus T.'s eyes brighten up. They almost twinkle.

"Bixby," says he, "what about that? Has there been an increase in the tonnage rate to the Corrugated?"

"I think so, sir," says Bixby. "I can look it up, sir."

"Ah!" says Runyon. "Bixby will look it up."

"He needn't," says Old Hickory. "It's been doubled, that's all. We had the notice last week. Torchy, did you—"

"Yep!" says I, shootin' the letter at him.

"Well, well!" says Runyon, after he's gazed at it. "There must have been some well founded cause for such an advance. Bixby, you must—"

"It's because you think you've got us in a hole," breaks in Old Hickory. "We've got to load our boats and you control the docks."

"Oh, yes!" chuckles Marcus T. "An unfortunate situation— for you. But I presume there are other dockage facilities available."

"If there were," says Mr. Ellins sarcastic, "do you think we would be paying you from three to five millions a year?"

"Bixby, I fear you must explain our position more fully," goes on Mr. Runyon.

"Oh, certainly," says Bixby. "I will have a full report prepared and—"

"Suppose you tell it to my secretary now," insists Old Hickory, glarin' menacin' at him.

"Do so, Bixby," says Marcus T.

"Why—er—you see," says Bixby, turnin' to me, "as I understand the case, the only outlet you have to deep water is over our tracks to—"

"What about them docks at Three Harbors?" I cuts in.

"Three Harbors?" repeats Bixby, starin' vague.

"Precisely," says Marcus T. "As the young man suggests, there is plenty of unemployed dockage at that point. But your ore tracks do not connect with that port."

"They would if we laid forty miles of rails, branchin' off at Tamarack Junction," says I. "That spur has all been surveyed and the right of way cleared."

"Ah!" exclaims Bixby, comin' to life again. "I remember now. Tamarack Junction. We hold a charter for a railroad from there to Three Harbors."

"You mean you did hold it," says I.

"I beg pardon?" says Bixby, gawpin'.

"It lapsed," says I, "eighteen months ago. Here's a copy, O. K.'d by a Minnesota notary public. See the date?"

"Allow me," says Mr. Runyon, reachin' for it.

Old Hickory gets up and rubbers over his shoulder. "By George!" says he. "It has lapsed, Runyon. Torchy, where's a map of—"

"Here you are," says I. "You'll see the branch line sketched in there. That would cut our haul about fifteen miles."

"And leave you with a lot of vacant ore docks on your hands, eh, Runyon?" puts in Old Hickory. "We could have those rails laid by the time the ice was out of the Soo. Well, well! Throws rather a new light on the situation, doesn't it?"

Marcus T. turns slow and fixes them keen eyes of his on Bixby the Busy.

"Hm-m-m!" says he. "It seems that we have overlooked a point, Bixby. Perhaps, though, you can offer—"

He can. Some shifty private sec, Bixby is.

"Your milk, sir," says he, grabbin' the tray and shovin' it in front of Runyon.

For a second or so the great Marcus T. eyes it indignant. Then his shoulders sag, the fire dies out of his eyes, and he takes the glass.

He's about the best trained plute I ever saw in captivity.

"And I think the doctor should take your temperature now," adds Bixby. "I will call him."

As he slips off toward the back end of the car Mr. Runyon lets out a sigh.

"It's no use, Ellins," says he. "One can't pamper a ruined digestion and still enjoy these friendly little business bouts. One simply can't. Name your own terms for continuing that terminal lease."

Old Hickory does prompt, for we don't want to buy rails at

the price they're bringin' now.

"And by the way, Runyon," says he, "may I ask what you pay your young man? I'm just curious."

"Bixby?" says Runyon. "Oh, twenty-five hundred."

"Huh!" says Mr. Ellins. "My secretary forgets my milk now and then, but he remembers such trifles as lapsed charters. He is drawing three thousand."

I hope Marcus T. didn't hear the gasp I lets out—I tried to smother it. And the first thing I does when we gets back into the limousine is to grin at the boss.

"Whaddye mean, three thousand?" says I.

"Dollars," says he. "Beginning to-day."

"Z-z-z-zing!" says I. "Going up, up! And there I was plannin' to take a special course in trained nursin', so I could hold my job."

CHAPTER IV

SWITCHING ARTS ON LEON

Oh, sure! We're coming along grand. Did you think we'd be heavin' the blue willow-ware at each other by this time? No. We've hardly displayed any before-breakfast dispositions yet.

Not that we confine ourselves to the coo vocabulary, or advertise any continuous turtle-dove act. Gettin' married ain't jellied our brains, I hope. Besides, we're busy. I've got a new gilt-edged job to fill, you know; and Vee, she has one of her own, too.

Well, I can't say that her scheme of runnin' a Boots, Limited, has mesmerized all New York into havin' its shoe-shinin' done out. There's something about this cloth top and white gaiter craze that's puttin' a crimp in her perfectly good plans. But she's doin' fairly well, and she don't have to think up ways of killin' time.

Course, we have a few other things to think about, too. Just learnin' how to live in New York is a merry little game all by itself. That's one of my big surprises. I'd thought all along it was so simple.

But say, we've been gettin' wise to a few facts this last month or so, for we've been tryin' to dope out which one of the forty-nine varieties of New York's home-sweet-home repertoire was the kind for us. I don't mean we've been changin' our street number, or testin' out different four-room-and-bath combinations. The studio apartment I got at a bargain suits first rate. It's the meal proposition.

First off, we decides gay and reckless that we'll breakfast and lunch in and take our dinners out. That listened well and seemed easy enough—until Vee got to huntin' up a two-handed, light-footed female party who could boil eggs without scorchin' the shells, dish up such things as canned salmon with cream sauce, and put a few potatoes through the French fry process, doublin' in bed-makin' and dust-chasin' durin' her spare time. That shouldn't call for any prize-winnin' graduate from a cookin' college, should it?

But say, the specimens that go in for general housework in this burg are a sad lot. I ain't goin' all through the list. I'll just touch lightly on Bertha.

She was a cheerful soul, even when she was servin' soggy potatoes or rappin' me in the ear with her elbow as she reached across to fill my water glass.

"He-he! Haw-haw! Oxcuse, Mister," was Bertha's repartee for such little breaks.

Course, I could plead with her for the umpteenth time to try pourin' from the button hand side, but it would have been simpler to have worn a head guard durin' meals.

And who would have the heart to put the ban on a yodel that begins in our kitchenette at 7 A.M., even on cloudy mornin's?

If Bertha had been No. 1, or even No. 2, she'd have had her passports handed her about the second mornin'; but, as she was the last of a punk half dozen, we tried not to mind her musical interludes. So at the end of three weeks her friendly relations with us were still unbroken, though most of the dishes were otherwise.

So you might have thought we'd been glad, when 6.30 P.M. came, to put on our things and join about a million or so other New Yorkers in findin' a dinner joint where the cooks and waiters made no claim to havin' an amateur standin'.

But, believe me, while my domestic instincts may be sproutin' late, they're comin' strong. I'm beginnin' to yearn for nourishment that I don't have to learn the French for or pick off'm a menu. I'd like to eat without bein' surrounded by three-chinned female parties with high blood pressure, or bein' stared at by pop-eyed old sports who're givin' some kittenish cloak model a bright evenin'. And Vee feels more or less the same way.

"Besides," says she, "I wish we could entertain some of our friends."

"Just what I was wishin'," says I. "Say, couldn't we find a few simple things in the cook-book that Bertha couldn't queer?"

"Such as canned baked beans and celery?" asks Vee, chucklin'. "And yet, if I stood by and read the directions to her—who knows?"

"Let's try her on the Piddies," I suggests.

Well, we did. And if the potatoes had been cooked a little more and the roast a little less, it wouldn't have been so bad.

The olives were all right, even if Bertha did forget to serve 'em until she brought in the ice cream. But then, the Piddies are used to little slips like that, havin' lived so long out in Jersey.

"You see," explains Vee to me afterwards, "Bertha was a bit flurried over her first dinner-party. She isn't much used to a gas oven, either. Don't you think we might try another?"

"Sure!" says I. "What are friends for, anyway? How about askin' Mr. and Mrs. Robert Ellins?"

"Oh, dear!" sighs Vee, lookin' scared. Then she is struck with a bright idea. "I'll tell you: we will rehearse the next one the night before."

"Atta girl!" says I. "Swell thought."

It was while she and Bertha was strugglin' over the cook-book, and gettin' advice from various sources, from housekeepin' magazines to the janitor's wife, that this Leon Battou party shows up with his sob hist'ry.

"Oh, Torchy!" Vee hails me with, as I come home from the office here the other evenin'. "What becomes of people when they're dispossessed—when they're put out on the street with their things, you know?"

"Why," says I, "they generally stay out until they can find a place where they can move in. Has anybody been threatenin' to chuck us out for not—"

"Silly!" says she. "It's the Battous."

"Don't know 'em," says I.

"But surely," goes on Vee, "you've seen him. He's that funny little old Frenchman who's always dodging in and out of the elevator with odd-looking parcels under his arm."

"Oh, yes!" says I. "The one with the twinklin' eyes and the curly iron-gray hair, who always bows so polite and shoots that bon-shure stuff at you. Him?"

It was.

It seems the agent had served notice on 'em that mornin'. They'd been havin' a grand pow-wow over it in the lower vestibule, when Vee had come along and got mixed up in the debate. She'd seen Mrs. Battou doin' the weep act on hubby's shoulder while he was tryin' to explain and makin' all sorts of promises. I expect the agent had heard such tales before. Anyway, he was kind of rough with 'em—at which Vee had sailed in and told him just what she thought.

"I'm sure you would have done the same, Torchy," says she.

"I might," says I, "if he hadn't been too husky. But what now?"

"I told them not to worry a bit," says Vee, "and that when you came home you would tell them what to do. You will, won't you, Torchy?"

Course, there was only one real sensible answer to that. Who was I, to step in casual and ditch a court order? But say, when the only girl in the universe tackles you with the clingin' clinch, hints that you're a big, brainy hero who can handle any proposition that's batted up to you—well, that's no time to be sensible.

"I'll do any foolish little thing you name," says I.

"Goody!" says Vee. "I just knew you would. We'll go right up and—"

"Just a sec," says I. "Maybe I'd better have a private talk with this Mr. Battou first off. Suppose you run up and jolly the old lady while he comes down here."

She agrees to that, and three minutes later I've struck a pose which is sort of a cross between that of a justice of the supreme court and a bush league umpire, while M. Leon Battou is sittin' on the edge of a chair opposite, conversin' rapid with both hands and a pair of eloquent eyebrows.

"But consider, monsieur," he's sayin'. "Only because of owing so little! Can they not wait until I have found some good customers for my paintings?"

"Oh! Then you're an artist, are you?"

"I have the honor," says he. "I should be pleased to have you inspect some of my—"

"It wouldn't help a bit," says I. "All I know about art is that as a rule it don't pay. Don't you do anything else?"

He hunches his shoulders and spreads out both hands.

"It is true, what you say of art," he goes on. "And so then I must do the decorating of walls—the wreaths of roses on the ceiling. That was my profession when we lived at Peronne. But here—there is trouble about the union. The greasy plumber will not work where I am, it seems. *Eh bien!* I am forced out. So I return to my landscapes. Are there not many rich Americans who pay well for such things?"

I waves him back into his chair.

"How'd you come to wander so far from this Peronne place?" says I.

"It was because of our son, Henri," says he. "You see, he preferred to be as my father was, a chef. I began that way, too. The Battous always do—a family of cooks. But I broke away. Henri would not. He became the pastry chef at the Hotel Gaspard in Peronne. And who shall say, too, that he was not an artist in his way? Yes, with a certain fame. At least, they heard here, in New York. You would not believe what they offered if he would leave Peronne. And after months of saying no he said yes. It was true. They paid as they promised—more. So Henri sends for us to come also. We found him living like a prince. Truly! For more than three years we enjoyed his good fortune.

"And then—*la guerre*! Henri must go to join his regiment. True, he might have stayed. But we talked not of that. It was for France. So he went, not to return. Ah, yes! At Ypres, after only three months in the trenches. Then I say to the little mother, 'Courage! I, Leon Battou, am still a painter. The art which has been as a pastime shall be made to yield us bread. You shall see.' Ah, I believed—then."

"Nothing doing, eh?" says I.

Battou shakes his head.

"Well," says I, "the surest bet just now would be to locate some wall-frescoin'. I'll see what can be done along that line."

"Ah, that is noble of you, young man," exclaims Battou. "It is wonderful to find such a friend. A thousand thanks! I will tell the little mother that we are saved."

With that he shakes me by both hands, gives me a bear hug, and rushes off.

Pretty soon Vee comes down with smiles in her eyes.

"I just knew you would find a way, Torchy," says she. "You don't know how happy you've made them. Now tell me all about it."

And say, I couldn't convince her I hadn't done a blamed thing but shoot a little hot air, not after I'd nearly gone hoarse explainin'.

"Oh, but you will," says she. "You'll do something."

Who could help tryin', after that? I tackles the agent with a proposition that Battou should work out the back rent, but he's a fish-eyed gink.

"Say," he growls out past his cigar, "if we tried to lug along every panhandling artist that wanted to graft rent off us, we'd be in fine shape by the end of the year, wouldn't we? Forget it."

"How about his art stuff?" I asks Vee, when I got back.

"Oh, utterly hopeless," says she. "But one can't tell him so. He doesn't know how bad it is. I suppose he is all right as a wall decorator. Do you know, Torchy, they must be in serious straits. Those two little rooms of theirs are almost bare, and I'm sure they've been living on cheese and crackers for days. What do you think I've done?"

"Sent 'em an anonymous ham by parcels post?" says I.

"No," says Vee. "I'm going to have them down to-night for the rehearsal dinner."

"Fine dope!" says I. "And if they survive bein' practiced on—"

But Vee has skipped off to the kitchenette without waitin' to hear the rest.

"Is this to be a reg'lar dress rehearsal?" I asks, when I comes home again. "Should I doll up regardless?"

Yes, she says I must. I was just strugglin' into my dinner coat, too, when the bell rings. I expect Vee had forgot to tell 'em that six-forty-five was our reg'lar hour. And say, M. Leon was right there with the boulevard costume—peg-top trousers, fancy vest, flowin' tie, and a silk tile. As for Madame Battou, she's all in gray and white.

I'd towed 'em into the studio, and was havin' 'em shed their things, when Vee bounces in out of the kitchenette and announces impetuous:

"Oh, Torchy! We've made a mess of everything. That horrid leg of lamb won't do anything but sozzle away in the pan; the string-beans have been scorched; and—oh, goodness!"

She'd caught sight of our guests.

"Please don't mind," says Vee. "We're not very good cooks, Bertha and I. We—we've spoiled everything, I guess."

She's tryin' to be cheerful over it. And she sure is a picture, standin' there with a big apron coverin' up most of her evenin' dress, and her upper lip a bit trembly.

"Buck up, Vee," says I. "Better luck next time. Chuck the whole shootin' match into the discards, and we'll all chase around to Roverti's and—"

"Bother Roverti's!" breaks in Vee. "Can't we ever have a decent dinner in our own home? Am I too stupid for that? And there's that perfectly gug-good l-l-l-leg of—of—"

"Pardon," says M. Battou, steppin' to the front; "but perhaps, if you would permit, I might assist with—with the lamb."

It's a novel idea, I admit. No wonder Vee gasps a little.

"Why not?" says I. "Course it ain't reg'lar, but if Mr. Battou wants to do some expert coachin', I expect you and Bertha could use it."

"Do, Leon," urges Madame Battou. "Lamb, is it? Oh, he is wonderful with lamb."

She hadn't overstated the case, either. Inside of two minutes he has his coat off, a bath towel draped over his fancy vest, and has sent Bertha skirmishin' down the avenue for garlic, cloves, parsley, carrots, and a few other things that had been overlooked, it seems.

Well, we stands grouped around the kitchenette door for a while, watchin' him resuscitate that pale-lookin' leg of lamb, jab things into it, pour stuff over it, and mesmerize the gas oven into doin' its full duty.

Once he gets started, he ain't satisfied with simply turnin' out the roast. He takes some string-beans and cuts 'em into shoelaces; he carves rosettes out of beets and carrots; he produces a swell salad out of nothing at all; and with a little flour and whipped cream he throws together some kind of puffy dessert that looked like it would melt in your mouth.

And by seven-thirty we was sittin' down to a meal such as you don't meet up with outside of some of them Fifth

Avenue joints where you have to own a head waiter before they let you in.

"Whisper, Professor," says I, "did you work a spell on it, or what?"

"Ah-h-h!" says Battou, chucklin' and rubbin' his hands together. "It is cooked *a la Paysan*, after the manner of Peronne, and with it is the sauce chateau."

"That isn't mere cookery," says Vee; "that's art."

It was quite a cheery evenin'. And after the Battous had gone, Vee and I asked each other, almost in chorus: "Do you suppose he'd do it again?"

"He will if I'm any persuader," says I. "Wouldn't it be great to spring something like that on Mr. Robert?"

And while I'm shavin' next mornin' I connect with the big idea. Do you ever get 'em that way? It cost me a nick under the ear, but I didn't care. While I'm usin' the alum stick I sketches out the scheme for Vee.

"But, Torchy!" says she. "Do you think he would—really?"

Before I can answer there's a ring at the door, and here is M. Leon Battou.

"The agent once more!" says he, producin' a paper. "In three days, it says. But you have found me the wall-painting, yes?"

"Professor," says I, "I hate to say it, but there's nothin' doing in the free-hand fresco line—absolutely."

He slumps into a chair, and that pitiful, hunted look settles in his eyes.

"Then—then we must go," says he.

"Listen, Professor," says I, pattin' him soothin' on the shoulder. "Why not can this art stuff, that nobody wants, and switch to somethin' you're a wizard at?"

"You—you mean," says he, "that I should—should turn chef? I—Leon Battou—in a big noisy hotel kitchen? Oh, but I could not. No, I could not!"

"Professor," says I, "the only person in this town that I know of who's nutty enough to want to hire a wall decorator reg'lar is me!"

"You!" gasps Battou, starin' around at our twelve by eighteen livin'-room.

I nods.

"What would you take it on for as a steady job?"

"Oh, anything that would provide for us," says he, eager. "But how—"

"That's just the point," says I. "When you wasn't paintin' could you cook a little on the side? Officially you'd be a decorator, but between times—Eh?"

He's a keen one, Mr. Battou.

"For so charming young people," says he, bowin' low, "it would be a great pleasure. And the little mother—ah, you should see what a manager she is! She can make a franc go farther. Could she assist also?"

"Could she!" exclaims Vee. "If she only would!"

Well, say, inside of half an hour we'd fixed up the whole deal, I'd armed Battou with a check to shove under the nose of that agent, and Vee had given Bertha her permanent release. And believe me, compared to what was put before Mr. and Mrs. Robert Ellins that evenin', the dress rehearsal dinner looked like Monday night at an actors' boardin'-house.

"I say," whispers Mr. Robert, "your cook must be a real artist."

"That's how he's carried on the family payroll," says I.

"Of course," says Vee afterwards, "while we can afford it, I suppose, it does seem scandalously extravagant for us to have cooking like that every day."

"Rather than have you worried with any more Bunglin' Berthas," says I, "I'd subsidize the whole of Peronne to come over. And just think of all I'll save by not havin' to buy my hat back from the coat-room boys every night."

CHAPTER V

A RECRUIT FOR THE EIGHT-THREE

Have you a shiny little set of garden tools in your home? Have we? Well, I should seed catalogue. Honest to goodness! Here! I can show you a local time-table and my commuter's ticket. How about that, eh, for me?

And I don't know now just what it was worked the sudden shift for us—the Battous, or our visit to the Robert Ellinses', or meetin' up with MacGregor Shinn, the consistent grouch.

It begun with window-boxes. Professor Leon Battou, our official wall decorator and actin' cook, springs 'em on me timid one day after lunch. It had been some snack, too— onion soup sprinkled with croutons and sprayed with grated cheese; calf's brains *au buerre noir*; a mixed salad; and a couple of gooseberry tarts with the demi-tasse. Say, I'm gettin' so I can eat in French, even if I can't talk it.

And while all that may listen expensive, I have Vee's word for it that since Madame Battou has been doin' the marketin' the high cost of livin' has been jarred off the roost. I don't know how accurate Professor Leon is at countin' up the calories in every meal, but I'm here to announce that he always produces something tasty, with no post-prandial regrets concealed in the bottom of the casserole.

"Professor," says I, "I've been a stranger to this burry brains style of nourishment a long time, but you can ring an encore on that whenever you like."

He smiles grateful, but shakes his head.

"Ah, Monsieur," says he,—oh, yes, just like that,—"but if I had the fresh chives, the—the *fin herbes*—ah, then you should see!"

"Well, can't Madame get what you need at the stores?" says I.

"But at such a price!" says Leon. "And of so discouraging a quality. While, if we had but a few handfuls of good soil in some small boxes by the windows—Come, I will show you. Here, and here, where the sun comes in the morning. I could secure them myself if you would not think them unlovely to have in view."

"How about it, Vee?" I asks. "Are we too proud to grow our soup greens on the premises?"

She says we ain't, so I tells Leon to breeze ahead with his hangin' garden. Course, I ain't lookin' for anything more'n a box on the ledge. But he's an ingenious old boy, Leon. With a hammer and saw and a few boxes from the grocery, he builds a rack that fits into one of the front windows; and the first thing I know, he has the space chuckful of shallow trays, and seeds planted in every one. A few days later, and the other window is blocked off similar. Also I get a bill from the florist for two bushels of dirt.

Well, our front windows did look kind of odd, and our view

out was pretty well barred off; but he had painted the things up neat, and he did all his waterin' and fussin' around early in the mornin', so we let it ride. When he starts in to use our bedroom windows the same way, though, I has to call him off.

"See here, Professor," says I, "you ain't mistakin' this studio apartment for a New Jersey truck-farm, are you! Besides, we have to keep them windows open at night, and your green stuff is apt to get nipped."

"Oh, but the night air is bad to breathe, Monsieur," says he.

"Not for us," says I. "Anyway, we're used to it, so I guess you'll have to lay off this bedroom garden business."

He takes away the boxes, but it's plain he's disappointed. I believe if I'd let him gone on he'd had cabbages growin' on the mantelpiece, a lettuce bed on the readin'-table, and maybe a potato patch on the fire-escape. I never knew gardenin' could be made such an indoor sport.

"Poor chap!" says Vee. "He has been telling me what wonderful things he used to raise when he lived in Peronne. Isn't there some way, Torchy, that we could give him more room?"

"We might rent the roof and glass it in for him," I suggests, "or get a permit to bridge over the street."

"Silly!" says she, rumplin' my red hair reckless.

That was about the time we was havin' some of that delayed winter weather, and it was touchin' to see Professor Battou nurse along them pale green shoots that he'd coaxed up in his window-boxes. Then it runs off warm and sunny again, just as we gets this week-end invite from Mr. Robert.

Course, I'd been out to his Long Island place before, but somehow I hadn't got excited over it. This time it's different. Vee was goin' along, for one thing. And I expect the fact that spring had come bouncin' in on us after a hard winter had something to do with our enthusiasm for gettin' out of town. You know how it is. For eleven months you're absolutely sure the city's the only place to live in, and you feel sorry for them near-Rubes who have to catch trains to get home. And then, all of a sudden, about this time of year, you get that restless feelin', and wonder what it is ails you. I think it struck Vee harder than it did me.

"Goody!" says she, when I tell her we're expected to go out Saturday noon and stay over until Monday mornin'. "It is real country out there, too, isn't it?"

"Blamed near an hour away," says I. "Ought to be, hadn't it?"

"I hope they have lilac bushes in bloom," says Vee. "Do you know, Torchy, if I lived in the country, I'd have those if nothing else. Wouldn't you?"

"I expect so," says I, "though I ain't doped out just what I would do in a case like that. It ain't seemed worth while. But if lilacs are the proper stunt for a swell country place, I'll bet Mr. Robert's got 'em."

By the time we'd been shot out to Harbor Hills station, though, I'd forgot whether it was lilacs or lilies-of-the-valley that Vee was particular about; for Mr. Robert goes along with us, and he's joshin' us about our livin' in a four-and-bath and sportin' a French chef.

"Really," says he, "to live up to him you ought to move into

Sewell Ford

a brewer's palace on Riverside Drive, at least."

"Oh, Battou would be satisfied if I'd lease Madison Square park for him, so he could raise onions," says I.

Which reminds Mr. Robert of something.

"Oh, I say!" he goes on. "You must see my garden. I'm rather proud of it, you know."

"Your garden!" says I, grinnin'. "You don't mean you've been gettin' the hoe and rake habit, Mr. Robert?"

Honest, that's the last thing you'd look for from him, for until he got married about the only times he ever strayed from the pavements was when he went yachtin'. But by the way he talks now you'd think farmer was his middle name.

"Now, over there," says he, after we've been picked up at the station by his machine and rolled off three or four miles, "over there I am raising a crop of Italian clover to plow in. That's a new hedge I'm setting out, too—hydrangeas, I think. It takes time to get things in shape, you see."

"Looks all right to me, as it is," says I. "You got a front yard big enough to get lost in."

Also the house ain't any small shack, with all its dormers and striped awnin's and deep verandas.

But it's too nice an afternoon to spend much time inside, and after we've found Mrs. Robert, Vee asks to be shown the garden.

"Certainly," says Mr. Robert. "I will exhibit it myself. That is—er—by the way, Gertrude, where the deuce is that garden of ours?"

Come to find out, it was Mrs. Robert who was the pie-plant and radish expert. She could tell you which rows was beets and which was corn without lookin' it up on her chart.

She'd been takin' a course in landscape-gardenin', too; and as she pilots us around the grounds, namin' the different bushes and things, she listens like a nursery pamphlet. And Vee falls for it hard.

"How perfectly splendid," says she, "to be able to plan things like that, and to know so many shrubs by their long names. But haven't you anything as common as lilacs!"

Mrs. Robert laughs and shakes her head.

"They were never mentioned in my course, you see," says she. "But our nearest neighbor has some wonderful lilac bushes. Robert, don't you think we might walk down the east drive and ask your dear friend Mr. MacGregor Shinn if he'd mind—"

"Decidedly no," cuts in Mr. Robert. "I'd much prefer not to trouble Mr. Shinn at all."

"Oh, very well," says Mrs. Robert. And then, turnin' to us: "We haven't been particularly fortunate in our relations with Mr. Shinn; our fault, no doubt."

But you know Vee. Half an hour later, when we've been left to ourselves, she announces:

"Come along, Torchy. I am going to find that east drive."

"It's a case of lilacs or bust, eh?" says I. "All right; I'm right behind you. But let's make it a sleuthy getaway, so they won't know."

We let on it was a risky stunt, slippin' out a side terrace door, dodgin' past the garage, and finally strikin' a driveway different from the one we'd come in by. We follows along until we fetches up by some big stone gateposts.

"There they are!" exclaims Vee. "Loads of them. And aren't they fragrant? Smell, Torchy."

"I am," says I, sniffin' deep. "Don't you hear me?"

"Yes; and that Mr. Shinn will too, if you're as noisy as that over it," says she. "I suppose that is where he lives. Isn't it the cutest little cottage?"

"It needs paint here and there," says I.

"I know," says Vee. "But look at that old Dutch roof with the wide eaves, and the recessed doorway, and the trellises on either side, and that big clump of purple lilacs nestling against the gable end. Oh, and there's a cunning little pond in the rear, just where it ought to be! I do wish we might go in and walk around a bit."

"Why not?" says I. "What would it hurt?"

"But that Shinn person," protests Vee, "might—might not—"

"Well, he couldn't any more'n shoo us off," says I, "and if he's nutty enough to do that after a good look at you, then he's hopeless."

"You absurd boy!" says Vee, squeezin' my hand. "Well, anyway, we might venture in a step or two."

As a matter of fact, there don't seem to be anyone in sight. You might almost think nobody lived there; for the new grass ain't been cut, the flower beds are full of dry weeds left over from last fall, and most of the green shutters are closed.

There's smoke comin' from the kitchen chimney, though, so we wanders around front, bringin' up under the big lilac bush. It's just covered with blossoms—a truck-load, I should say; and it did seem a shame, Vee bein' so strong for 'em, that she couldn't have one little spray.

"About a quarter a bunch, them would be on Broadway," says I, diggin' up some change. "Well, here's where Neighbor Shinn makes a sale."

And, before Vee can object, I've snapped off the end of a twig.

I'd just dropped the quarter in an envelop and was stickin' it on the end of the broken branch, when the front door opens, and out dashes this tall gink with the rusty Vandyke and the hectic face. Yep, it's a lurid map, all right. Some of it might have been from goin' without a hat in the wind and weather, for his forehead and bald spot are just as high-colored as the rest; but there's a lot of temper tint, too, lightin' up the tan, and the deep furrows between the eyes shows it ain't an uncommon state for him to be in. Quite a husk he is, costumed in a plaid golf suit, and he bores down on us just as gentle as a tornado.

"I say, you!" he calls out. "Stop where you are."

"Don't hurry," says I. "We'll wait for you."

"Ye will, wull ye!" he snarls, as he comes stampin' up in front of us. "Ye'd best. And what have ye there, Miss? Hah!

Pickin' me posies, eh? And trespassin', too."

"That's right," says I. "Petty larceny and breakin' and enterin'. I'm the guilty party."

"I'm sure there's nothing to make such a fuss about," says Vee, eyin' him scornful.

"Oh, ho!" says he. "It's a light matter, I suppose, prowling around private grounds and pilfering? I ought to be taking it as a joke, eh? Don't ye know, you two, I could have you taken in charge for this?"

"Breeze ahead, then," says I. "Call the high sheriff. Only let's not get all foamed up over it, Mr. MacGregor Shinn."

"Ha!" says he. "Then ye know who I am? Maybe you're stopping up at the big house?"

"We are guests of Mr. Ellins, your neighbor," puts in Vee.

"He's no neighbor of mine," snaps Shinn. "Not him. His bulldog worries me cat, his roosters wake me up in the morning, and his Dago workmen chatter about all day long. No, I'll not own such a man as neighbor. Nor will I have his guests stealing my posies."

"Then take it," says Vee, throwing the lilac spray on the ground.

"You'll find a quarter stuck on the bush," says I. "Sorry, MacGregor, we couldn't make a trade. The young lady is mighty fond of lilacs."

"Is she, now?" says Shinn, still scowlin' at us.

"And she thinks your place here is pretty cute," I adds.

"It's a rotten hole," says he.

"Maybe you're a poor judge," says I. "If it was fixed up a bit I should think it might be quite spiffy."

"What call has an old bachelor to be fixing things up?" he demands. "What do I care how the place looks? And what business is it of yours, anyway?"

"Say, you're a consistent grouch, ain't you?" says I, givin' him the grin. "What's the particular trouble—was you toppin' your drive to-day?"

"Slicin', mon," says he. "Hardly a tee shot found the fairway the whole round. And then you two come breaking me bushes."

"My error," says I. "But you should have hung out a sign that you was inside chewin' nails."

"I was doing nothing of the kind," says he. "I was waiting for that grinning idiot, Len Hung, to give me me tea."

"Well, don't choke over it when you do get it," says I. "And if you ain't ready to sic the police on us we'll be trotting along back."

"Ye wull not," says MacGregor; "ye'll have tea with me."

It sounds like a threat, and I can see Vee gettin' ready to object strenuous. So I gives her the nudge.

I expect it's because I'm so used to Old Hickory's blowin' out a fuse that I don't duck quicker when a gas-bomb disposition begins to sputter around. They don't mean half of it, these furious fizzers.

Sometimes it's sciatica, more often a punk digestion, and seldom pure cussedness. If you don't humor 'em by comin' back messy yourself, but just jolly 'em along, they're apt to work out of it. And I'd seen sort of a human flicker in them blue-gray eyes of MacGregor Shinn's.

"Vee," says I, "our peevish friend is invitin' us to take tea with him. Shall we chance it?"

And you know what a good sport Vee is. She lets the curve come into her mouth corners again, both of her cheek dimples show, and she shoots a quizzin' smile at Mr. Shinn.

"Does he say it real polite?" she asks.

"Na," says MacGregor. "But there'll be hot scones and marmalade."

"M-m-m-m!" says Vee. "Let's, Torchy."

It's an odd finish to an affair that started so scrappy. Not that Shinn reverses himself entirely, or turns from a whiskered golf grump into a stage fairy in spangled skirts. He goes right on with his growlin' and grumblin'—about the way his Chink cook serves the tea, about havin' to live in a rotten hole like Harbor Hills, about everything in general. But a great deal of it is just to hear himself talk, I judge.

We had a perfectly good high tea, and them buttered scones with marmalade couldn't be beat. Also he shows us all over the house, and Vee raves about it.

"Look, Torchy!" says she. "That glimpse of water from the

living-room windows. Isn't that dear? And one could have such a wonderful garden beyond. Such a splendid big fireplace, too. And what huge beams in the ceiling! It's a very old house, isn't it, Mr. Shinn?"

"The rascally agent who sold it to me said it was," says MacGregor, "but I wouldn't believe a word of his on any subject. 'Did I ask you for an old house, at all?' I tells him. For what I wanted was just a place where I could live quiet, and maybe have me game of golf when I wanted it. But here I've gone off me game; and, besides, the country's no place to live quiet in. I should be in town, so I should, like any decent white man. I've a mind to look up a place at once. Try another scone, young lady."

So it was long after six before we got away, and the last thing MacGregor does is to load Vee down with a whole armful of lilac blossoms.

I suppose Mr. and Mrs. Robert thought we'd been makin' a wholesale raid when they saw us comin' in with the plunder. Mrs. Robert almost turns pale.

"Mercy!" says she. "You don't mean to say you got all those from our neighbor's bushes, do you?"

"Uh-huh," says I. "We've been mesmerizin' MacGregor. He's as tame a Scot now as you'd want to see."

They could hardly believe it, and when they heard about our havin' tea with him they gasped.

"Of all persons!" says Mrs. Robert. "Why, he has been glaring at us for a year, and sending us the most bristling messages. I don't understand."

Mr. Robert, though, winks knowin'.

"Some of Torchy's red-headed diplomacy, I suspect," says he. "I must engage you to make our peace with MacGregor."

That's all we saw of him, though, durin' our stay. For one thing, we was kept fairly busy. I never knew you could have so much fun in the country. Ever watch a bunch of young ducks waddlin' about? Say, ain't they a circus! And them fluffy little chicks squabblin' over worms. Honest, I near laughed myself sick. Vee was for luggin' some of 'em home to the apartment. But she was thrilled over 'most everything out there, from the fat robins on the lawn to the new leaves on the trees.

And, believe me, when we gets back to town again, our studio apartment seems cramped and stuffy. We talked over everything we'd seen and done at the Ellinses'.

"That's really living, isn't it?" says Vee.

"Why not," says I, "with a twenty-room house, and grounds half as big as Central Park?"

"I know," says Vee. "But a little place like Mr. Shinn's would be large enough for us."

"I expect it would," says I. "You don't really think you'd like to live out there, do you, though?"

"Wouldn't I!" says Vee, her eyes sparklin'. "I'd love it."

"What would you do all day alone?" I suggests.

"I'd raise ducks and chickens and flowers," says Vee. "And Leon could have a garden. Just think!"

Yep—I thought. I must have kept awake hours that night, tryin' not to. And the more I mulled it over—Well, in the mornin' I had a talk with Mr. Robert, after which I got busy with the long-distance 'phone. I didn't say anything much at lunch about what I'd done, but around three o'clock I calls up the apartment.

"I'm luggin' home someone to dinner," says I. "Guess who?"

Vee couldn't.

"MacGregor the grouch," says I.

"Really!" says Vee. "How funny!"

"It's part of the plot," says I. "Tell the Professor to spread himself on the eatings, and have the rooms all fixed up slick."

Vee says she will. And she does. MacGregor falls for it, too. You should have seen him after dinner, leanin' back comfortable in our biggest chair, sippin' his coffee, and puffin' one of Old Hickory's special perfectos that I'd begged for the occasion.

And still I didn't let on. What I'm after is to have him spring the proposition on me. Just before he's ready to go, too, he does.

"I say," says he casual, "this isn't such a bad hole you have here."

"Perfectly rotten," says I.

"Then we might make a trade," says he. "What?"

"There's no tellin'," says I. "You mean a swap, as things stand?"

"That's it," says he. "I'm no hand for moving rubbish about."

"Me either," says I. "But if you mean business, suppose you drop in to-morrow at the office, about ten-thirty, and talk it over."

"Very well," says MacGregor. "I'll stop in town to-night."

"Oh, Torchy!" says Vee, after he's gone. "Do—do you suppose he will—really?"

"You're still for it, eh?" says I. "Sure, now?"

"Oh, it would be almost too good to be true," says she. "That could be made just the dearest place!"

"Yes," says I; "but my job is to talk MacGregor into lettin' it go cheap, or else we can't afford to touch it."

Well, I can't claim it was all my smooth work that did the trick, for MacGregor had bought the place at a bargain first off, and now he was anxious to unload. Still, he hadn't been born north of Glasgow for nothing. But the figures Mr. Robert said would be about right I managed to shade by twenty per cent., and my lump invoice of that old mahogany of ours maybe was a bit generous. Anyway, when I goes home that night I tosses Vee a long envelop.

"What's this?" says she.

"That's your chicken permit," says I. "All aboard for Lilac Lodge! Gee! I wonder should I grow whiskers, livin' out there?"

CHAPTER VI

TORCHY IN THE GAZINKUS CLASS

I expect I'll get used to it all in time. This rural stuff, I mean. But it ain't goin' to come easy. When you've been brought up to think of home as some place where you've got a right to leave your trunk as long as you pay the rent prompt,—a joint where you have so many square feet of space on a certain floor, and maybe eight or ten inches of brick and plaster between you and a lot of strangers,—and then all of a sudden you switch to a whole house that's all yours, with gobs of land all around it, and trees and bushes and things that you can do what you like with—well, it's sort of staggerin' at first.

Why, the day Vee and I moved into this Harbor Hills place that I'd made the swift trade for with MacGregor Shinn, we just had our baggage dumped in the middle of the livin'-room, chucked our wraps on some chairs, and went scoutin' around from one room to another for over an hour, kind of nutty and excited.

"Oh, look, Torchy!" Vee would exclaim about twice a minute when she discovered something new.

You know, we'd been in the house only once before, and

then we'd looked around just casual. And if you want to find out how little you really see when you think you're lookin', you want to make a deal like that once—buy a joint just as it stands, and then, a few days after, camp down in it and tot up what you've really got. Why, say, you'd 'most thought we'd been blindfolded that first time.

Course, this was different. Now we was takin' stock, you might say, of the things we was goin' to live with. And, believe me, I never had any idea I'd ever own such a collection, or so big a slice of the U. S. A.

"Only think, Torchy," says Vee, after we've made the rounds inside. "Ten rooms, just for us!"

"Twelve, countin' the cellar and attic," says I. "But there's more outside, ain't there?"

Yep, there was. There was an old stable that had been turned into a garage, with a couple of rooms finished off upstairs. Then there was a carriage shed, with more rooms over that, also a chicken house beyond. And stowed away in odd corners was all kinds of junk that might be more or less useful to have: a couple of lawn-mowers, an old sleigh hoisted up on the rafters of the carriage house, a weird old buggy, a plow, a grindstone, a collection of old chairs and sofas that had seen better days, a birch-bark canoe—things like that.

Then there was our lily pond. We had to walk all round that, poke in with a pole to see how deep it might be, and wonder if there was any fish in it. On beyond was some trees—apple and pear and cherry, accordin' to Vee, and 'way at the back a tall cedar hedge.

"Why, it's almost an estate," says Vee. "Nearly five acres,

you know. How does it seem, Torchy, to think that all this is ours?"

"How?" says I. "Why, I feel like I was the Grand Gazinkus of Gazook."

But, at that, my feelin's wa'n't a marker to the emotions Professor Leon Battou, our artist-chef, manages to work up. He's so tickled at gettin' back to the country and away from the city, where him and Madame Battou come so near starvin' on the street, that he goes skippin' around like a sunshine kid, pattin' the trees, droppin' down on his hands and knees in the grass to dig up dandelions, and keepin' up a steady stream of explosive French and rapid-fire English.

"Ah, but it is all so good!" says he. "*Le bleu ciel, les fleurs, les oiseaux! C'est bonne, tres bonne. Ne c'est pas?*"

"I expect it is, Leon," says I. "Although I might not state it just that way myself. Picked out a spot yet for your garden?"

Foolish question! That was his first move, after taking a glance at the particular brand of cook-stove he'd got to wrestle with. Just to the left of the kitchen wing is a little plot shut in by privet bushes and a trellis, which is where he says the *fine herbes* are meant to grow. He tows us around there and exhibits it chesty. Mostly it's full of last year's weeds; but he explains how he will soon have it in shape. And for the next week the only way we ever got any meals cooked was because Madame Battou used to go drag him in by the arm and make him quit diggin' long enough to hash up some of them tasty dishes for us.

If all amateur gardeners are apt to go so dippy over it, I hope I don't catch the disease. No danger, I guess. I made my stab at it about the third day, when Vee wanted some ground spaded up for a pansy bed. And say, in half an hour, there, I'd worked up enough palm blisters and backache to last me a month. It may seem sport to some people, but to me it has all the ear-marks of plain, hard work, such as you can indulge in reg'lar by carryin' a foldin' dinner-pail and lettin' yourself out to a padrone.

Leon, though, just couldn't seem to let it alone. He almost made a vice of it, to my mind. Why, say, he's out there at first crack of day, whenever that is; and in the evenin', as soon as he has served dinner, he sneaks out to put in a few more licks, and stays until it's so dark he can hardly find his way back.

You know all them window-boxes he had clutterin' up the studio apartment. Well, he insists on cratin' every last one of 'em and expressin' 'em along; and now he has all that alleged lettuce and parsley and carrots and so on set out in neat little rows; and when he ain't sprinklin' 'em with the hose or dosin' 'em with fertilizer, he's out there ticklin' 'em with a rake.

"Gee!" says I. "I thought all you had to do to a garden was just to chuck in the seeds and let 'em grow. But accordin' to your method it would be less trouble bringin' up a pair of twins."

"Ah-h-h-h!" says he. "But monsieur has not the passion for growing green things."

"Thanks be, then," says I. "It would land me in the liniment ward if I had."

I must say, though, that Vee's 'most as bad with her flowers. Honest, when she shows me where she's planned to have this and that, and hints that I can get busy durin' my spare time with the spade, I almost wished we was back in town.

"What?" I gasps. "Want me to excavate all that? Hal-lup!"

"Pooh!" says Vee. "It will do you good."

Maybe she thought so. But I knew it wouldn't. So I chases up the hill to the Ellins place, and broke in on Mr. Robert just as he's finishin' breakfast.

"Say," says I, "you ain't got a baby-grand steam-shovel or anything like that around the place, have you?"

He says he's sorry, but he ain't. When he hears what I'm up against, though, he comes to the rescue noble by lendin' me one of his expert Dago soil-disturbers, at $1.75 per—and with Vee bossin' him she got the whole job done in half a day. After that I begun to enjoy gardenin' a bit more. I'm gettin' to be a real shark at it, too. And ambitious! You ought to hear me.

"How about havin' a couple more lanes of string-beans laid out?" I suggests. "And maybe a few hundred mounds of green corn, eh?"

And then I can watch Joe start the enterprise with a plow and an old white horse, and I can go to the office feelin' that, no matter how much I seem to be soldierin', as a matter of fact I'm puttin' in a full day's work. When I get back in the afternoon, the first thing I want to see is how much I've got done.

Not that I'm able to duck all kinds of labor that way. Believe me, a country place is no loafin' spot, especially when it's new, or you're new to it. Vee tends to that. Say, that girl can think up more odd forms of givin' me exercise than a bunch of football coaches—movin' bureaus, hangin' pictures, puttin' up curtain-rods, fixin' door-catches, and little things like that.

Up to a few weeks ago all I knew about saws and screw-drivers and so on was that they were shiny things displayed in the hardware store windows. But if I keep on tacklin' all the odd jobs she sics me on to, I'll be able to qualify pretty soon as a boss carpenter, a master plumber, and an expert electrician.

Course, I gouge myself now and then. My knuckles look like I'd been mixin' in a food riot, and I've spoiled two perfectly good suits of clothes. But I can point with pride to at least three doors that I've coaxed into shuttin', I've solved the mystery of what happens to a window-weight when the sash-cord breaks, and I've rigged up two drop-lights without gettin' myself electrocuted or askin' any advice from Mr. Edison.

Which reminds me that what I can't seem to get used to about the country is the poor way it's lighted up at night. You know, our place is out a couple of miles from the village and the railroad station; and, while we got electric bulbs enough in the house, outside there ain't a lamp-post in sight. Dark! Say, after 8 P.M. you might as well be livin' in a sub-cellar with the sidewalk gratin' closed. Honest, the only glim we can see from our front porch is a flicker from the porte cochere at the Ellinses' up on the hill, and most of that is cut off by trees and lilac bushes.

Vee don't seem to mind, though. These mild evenin's recent, she's dragged me out after dinner for a spell and made me sit with her watchin' for the moon to come up. I do it, but it ain't anything I'm strong for. I can't see the percentage in starin' out at nothing at all but black space and guessin' where the driveway is or what them dark streaks are. Then, there's so many weird sounds I can't account for.

"What's all that jinglin' going on?" I asks the other evenin'.

"Sounds like a squad of junkmen comin' up the pike."

"Silly!" says Vee. "Frogs, of course."

"Oh!" says I.

Then I listens some more, until something else breaks loose. It's sort of a cross between the dyin' moan of a gyastacutus and the whine of a subway express roundin' a sharp curve.

"For the love of Pete," I breaks out, "what do you call that?"

Vee chuckles. "Didn't you see the calf up at Mr. Robert's?" she asks. "Well, that's the old cow calling to him."

"If she feels as bad as that," says I, "I wish she'd wait until mornin' to express herself. That's the most doleful sound I ever heard. Come on; let's go in while you tinkle out something lively and cheerin' on the piano."

I never thought I was one of the timid kind, either. Course, I'm no Carnegie hero, or anything like that; but I've always managed to get along in the city without developin' a case of nerves. Out here, though, it's different. Two or three evenin's now I've felt almost jumpy, just over nothing at all, it seems.

Maybe that's why I didn't show up any better, here the other night, when Vee rings in this silent alarm on me. I was certainly poundin' my ear industrious when gradually I gets the idea that someone is shakin' me by the shoulders. It's Vee.

"Torchy," she whispers husky. "Get up."

"Eh?" says I, pryin' my eyes open reluctant. "Get up? Wha-wha' for?"

"Oh, don't be stupid about it," says she. "I've been trying to rouse you for five minutes. Please get up and come to the window."

"Nothing doing," says I snugglin' into the pillow again. "I— I'm busy."

"But you must," says she. "Listen. I think someone is prowling around the house."

"Let 'em ramble, then," says I. "What do we care?"

"But suppose it's a—a burglar?" she whispers.

I'll admit that gives me a goose-fleshy feelin' down the spine. It's such a disturbin' word to have sprung on you in the middle of the night.

"Let's not suppose anything of the sort," says I.

"But I'm sure I saw someone just now, when I got up to fix the shade," insists Vee. "Someone who stepped out into the moonlight right there, between the shadows of those two trees. Then he disappeared out that way. Come and look."

Well, I was up by then, and half awake, so I tries to peer out into the back yard. I'm all for grantin' a general alibi, though.

"Maybe you was only dreamin', Vee," says I. "Anyway, let's wait until mornin', and then—"

"There!" she breaks in excited. "Just beyond the garden trellis. See?"

Yep. There's no denyin' that someone is sneakin' around out there. First off I thought it might be a female in a white skirt and a raincoat; but when we gets the head showin' plain above some bushes we can make out a mustache.

"It's a man!" gasps Vee, clutchin' me by the sleeve.

"Uh-huh," says I. "So it is."

"Well?" says Vee.

I expect that was my cue to come across with the bold and noble acts. But, somehow, I didn't yearn to dash out into the moonlight in my pajamas and mix in rough with a total stranger. But I didn't mean to give it away if I could help it.

"Got a nerve, ain't he?" says I. "Let's wait; maybe he'll fall into the pond."

"How absurd!" says Vee. "No; we must do something right away."

"Of course," says I. "I'll shout and ask him what the blazes he thinks he's doin'."

"Don't," says Vee. "There may be others—in the house. And before you let him know you see him, you ought to be armed. Get your revolver."

At that I just gawped at Vee, for she knows well enough I don't own anything more deadly than a safety razor, and that all the gun-play I ever indulged in was once or twice at a Coney Island shootin' gallery where I slaughtered a clay pipe by aimin' at a glass ball.

"Whaddye mean, revolver?" I asks.

"S-s-s-sh!" says she. "There's that Turkish pistol, you know, that Mr. Shinn left hanging over the mantel in the living-room."

"Think it's loaded?" I whispers.

"It might be," says Vee. "Anyway, it's better than nothing. Let's get it."

"All right," says I. "Soon as I get something on. Just a sec."

So I jumps into a pair of trousers and a coat and some bath slippers, while Vee throws on a dressin'-sack. We feels our way sleuthy downstairs, and after rappin' my shins on a couple of rockers I gets down the old pistol. It's a curious, wicked-lookin' antique about two feet long, with a lot of carvin' and silver inlay on the barrel. I'd never examined the thing to see how it worked, but it feels sort of comfortin' just to grip it in my hand. We unlocks the back door easy.

"Now you stay inside, Vee," says I, "while I go scoutin' and—"

"No indeed," says Vee. "I am going too."

"But you mustn't," I insists.

"Hush!" says she. "I shall."

And she did. So we begins our first burglar hunt as a twosome, and I must say there's other sports I enjoy more. Out across the lawn we sneaks, steppin' as easy as we can, and keepin' in the shadow most of the time.

"Guess he must have skipped," says I.

"But he was here only a moment ago," says Vee. "Don't you

know, we saw him—Oh, oh!"

I don't blame her for gaspin'. Not twenty feet ahead of us, crouchin' down in the cabbage patch, is the villain. Just why he should be tryin' to hide among a lot of cabbage plants not over three inches high, I don't stop to think. All I knew was that here was someone prowlin' around at night on my premises, and all in a flash I begins to see red. Swingin' Vee behind me, I unlimbers the old pistol and cocks it. I didn't care whether this was the open season for burglars or not. I wanted to get this one, and get him hard.

Must have been a minute or more that I had him covered, tryin' to steady my arm so I could keep the muzzle pointed straight at his back, when all of a sudden he lifts his right hand and begins scratchin' his ear. Somehow, that breaks the spell. Why should a burglar hump himself on his hands and knees in a truck patch and stop to scratch his ear?

"Hey, you!" I sings out real crisp.

Maybe that ain't quite the way to open a line of chat with a midnight marauder. I've been kidded about it some since; but at the time it sounded all right. And it had the proper effect. He comes up on his toes with his hands in the air, like he was worked by springs.

"That's right; keep your paws up," says I. "And, remember, if you go to makin' any funny moves—"

"Why, Torchy!" exclaims Vee, grabbin' my shootin' arm. "It's Leon!"

"Wha-a-a-at!" says I, starin' at this wabbly party among the coldslaw.

But it's Professor Battou, all right. He's costumed in a night-shirt, an old overcoat, and a pair of rubbers; and he certainly does look odd, standin' there in the moonlight with his elbows up and his knees knockin' one another.

"Well, well, Leon!" says I, sighin' relieved. "So it's you, is it? And we had you all spotted as a second-story worker. All right; you don't need to hold the pose any longer. But maybe you'll tell us what you're crawlin' around out here in the garden for at this time of night."

He tried to, but he's had such a scare thrown into him that his conversation works are all gummed up. After we've led him into the house, though, and he's had a drink of spring water, he does a little better.

"It was to protect the cabbages, monsieur," says he.

"Eh?" says I. "Protect 'em from what?"

"There is a wicked worm," says Leon, "which does his evil work in the night. Ah, such a sly beast! And so destructive! Just at the top of the young root he eats—snip, snip! And in the morning I find that two, four, sometimes six tender plants he has cut off. I am enrage. 'Ha!' I say. 'I will discover you yet at your mischief.' So I cannot sleep for thinking. But I had found him; yes, two. And I was searching for more when monsieur—"

"Yes, I know," says I. He's glancin' worried at the old pistol I'm still holdin' in my hand. "My error, Leon. I might have guessed. And as the clock's just strikin' three, I think we'd all better hit the hay again. Come on, Vee; it's all over."

And, in spite of that half hour or so of time out, I was up earlier than usual in the mornin'. I had a little job to do that

I'd planned out before I went to sleep again. As soon as I'm dressed I slips downstairs, takes that Turkish pistol, and chucks it into the middle of the pond. I'll never know whether it was loaded or not. I don't want to know. For if it had been—Well, what's the use?

Comin' back in through the kitchen, I finds Leon busy dishin' up toast and eggs. He glances at me nervous, and then hangs his head. But he gets out what he has to say man fashion.

"I trust monsieur is not displeased," says he. "It was not wise for me to walk about at night. But those wicked worms! Still, if monsieur desires, it shall not occur again. I ask pardon."

"Now, that's all right, Leon," says I soothin'. "Don't worry. When it comes to playin' the boob act, I guess we split about fifty-fifty. I'd a little rather you didn't, but if you must hunt the wicked worm at night, why, go to it. You won't run any more risk of being shot up by me. For I've disarmed."

CHAPTER VII

BACK WITH CLARA BELLE

And me kiddin' myself I was fairly well parlor-broke. It seems not. You'd 'most think, though, I'd had enough front-room trainin' to stand me through in a place like Harbor Hills. I had a wild idea, too, that when we moved into the country we'd tagged the reg'lar social stuff good-by.

That was a poor hunch. I'm just discoverin' that there's more tea fights and dinner dances and such goin's on out here in the commuter zone than in any five blocks of Fifth Avenue you can name. And it seems that anywhere within ten miles of this Piping Rock Club brings you into the most active sector. So here we are, right in the thick of things.

At that, I expect it might have been quite some time before we was bothered any if it hadn't been for our bein' sort of backed by the Robert Ellinses. As their friends we're counted in right off the reel. I've been joshed into lettin' my name go on the waitin' list at the Country Club; I'm allowed to subscribe to this and that; some of the neighbors have begun payin' first calls on Vee.

So I might have had sense enough to watch my step. Yet, here the other afternoon, when I makes an early getaway from the Corrugated and hops off the 5:17, I dashes across the back lots and comes into our place by the rear instead of the front drive. You see, I'd been watchin' a row of string-beans we had comin' along, and I wanted to spring the first ones on Vee. Sure enough, I finds three or four pods 'most big enough to eat; so I picks 'em and goes breezin' into the house, wavin' em gleeful.

"Oh, Vee!" I sings out, openin' the terrace door. "Come have a look."

And, as she don't appear on the jump, I keeps on into the livin'-room and calls:

"Hey! What do you know about these? Beans! Perfectly good—"

Well, that's as far as I gets, for there's Vee, sittin' behind the silver tea-urn, all dolled up; and Leon, in his black coat, holdin' a plate of dinky little cakes; and a couple of strange ladies starin' at me button-eyed. I'd crashed right into the midst of tea and callers.

Do I pull some easy johndrew lines and exit graceful? Not me. My feet was glued to the rug.

"Beans!" says I, grinnin' simple and danglin' the specimens. "Perfectly good string—"

Then I catches the eye of the stiff-necked dame with the straight nose and the gun-metal hair. No, both eyes, it was; and a cold, suspicious, stabby look is what they shoots my way. No wonder I chokes off the feeble-minded remarks and turns sort of panicky to Vee, half expectin' to find her blushin' painful or signalin' me to clear out. Nothing like that from Vee, though.

"Not ours, Torchy?" says she, slidin' out from behind the tea-table and rushin' over. "Not our very own?"

"Uh-huh!" says I. "Just picked 'em."

At which the other caller joins in unexpected.

"From your own garden?" says she. "How interesting! Oh, do show them to me."

"Why, sure," says I. "Guess we're doin' our bit, ain't we?"

She's a wide, dumpy-built old girl, and dressed sort of freaky. Also her line of talk is a kind of purry, throaty gush that's almost too soothin' to be true. But anybody who makes only half a bluff at being interested in our garden wins us. And not until she's inspected our first string-beans through her gold lorgnette, and remarked twice more how wonderful it was for us to raise anything like that, does it occur to Vee to introduce me proper to both ladies.

The tall, stiff-necked dame turns out to be Mrs. Pemberton Foote. Honest! Could you blame her for bein' jarred when I come bouncin' in with garden truck?

Think of it! Why, she's one of the super-tax brigade and moves among the smartest of the smart-setters. And Pemmy, he's on the polo team, you know.

Oh, reg'lar people, the Pembroke Footes are. And the very fact that Mrs. Foote is here callin' on Vee ought to have me thrilled to the bone.

Yet all I got sense enough to do is wave half-grown string-beans at her, and then sit by gawpy, balancin' a cup of tea on my knee, and watch her apply the refrigeratin' process to the dumpy old girl whose name I didn't quite catch. Say, but she does it thorough and artistic. Only two or three times did the dumpy one try to kick in on the chat, and when she does, Mrs. Pemmy rolls them glittery eyes towards her slow, givin' her the up-and-down like she was some kind of fat worm that had strayed in from the cucumber bed.

Can't these women throw the harpoon into each other ruthless, though? Why, you could see that old girl fairly squirm when she got one of them assault-and-battery glances. Her under lip would quiver a bit, she'd wink hard three or four times, and then she'd sort of collapse, smotherin' a sigh and not finishin' what she'd started out to say. She did want to be so folksy, too.

Course, she's an odd-lookin' party, with that bucket-shaped lid decorated with pale green satin fruit, and the piles of thick blondine hair that was turnin' gray, and her foolish big eyes with the puffy rolls underneath and the crows'-feet in the corners. And of course anybody with ankles suggestin' piano legs really shouldn't go in for high-tide skirts and white silk stockin's with black butterflies worked on 'em. Should they?

Still, she'd raved over our string-beans, so when she makes a last fluttery try at jimmyin' her way into the conversation, and Mrs. Foote squelches her prompt again, and she gives up for good, it's me jumpin' snappy to tow her out and tuck her in the limousine. Havin' made my escape, I stays outside until after Mrs. Pemmy has gone too, which don't happen for near half an hour later. But when I hears the front door shut on her, I sidles in at the back.

"Zowie!" says I. "You must have made more of a hit with our swell neighbor than I did, Vee."

Vee smiles quizzin' and shrugs her shoulders.

"I'm not so sure," says she. "I almost feel as though we had been visited by the Probation Officer, or someone like that."

"How do you mean?" says I.

"Of course," she goes on, "Mrs. Foote did not actually say that we were on trial socially, but she hinted as much. And she made it quite plain that unless we got started in the right set our case would be utterly hopeless."

"Just think of that!" says I. "Real sweet of her, eh? Sort of inspector general, is she? You should have asked her to show her badge, though."

"Oh, there's no doubt that she speaks with authority," says Vee. "She wasn't snippy about it, either. And chiefly she was trying to warn me against Mrs. Ben Tupper."

"The old girl with the pelican chin and the rovin' eyes?" I asks. "What's the matter with her besides her looks?"

Well, accordin' to Mrs. Pemmy Foote, there was a lot. She had a past, for one thing. She was a pushing, presumptuous person, for another. And, besides, this Benjamin Tupper party—the male of the species—was wholly impossible.

"You know who he is," adds Vee. "The tablet man."

"What?" says I. "'Tupper's Tablets for Indigestion—on Everybody's Tongue.' Him?"

Vee nods. "And they live in that barny stucco house just as you turn off Sagamore Boulevard—the one with the hideous red-tiled roof and the concrete lions in front."

"Goodness Agnes!" says I. "Folks have been indicted for less than that. I've seen Tupper, too; someone pointed him out goin' in on the express only the other mornin'. Looks like a returned Nihilist who'd been nominated in one of the back wards of Petrograd to run for the Duma on a free-vodka platform. He's got wiry whiskers that he must trim with a pair of tin-shears, tufts in his ears, and the general build of a performin' chimpanzee. Oh, he's a rare one, Tupper."

"Then," says Vee, sort of draggy, "I—I suppose Mrs. Foote is right. It's too bad, for that Mrs. Tupper did seem such a friendly old soul. And I shall feel so snobbish if I don't return her call."

"Huh!" says I. "I don't see why Mrs. Pemmy couldn't let you find out about her for yourself. Even if the old girl don't belong, what's the use bein' so rough with her?"

"Do you know, Torchy," says Vee, "I felt that way about it when Mrs. Foote was snubbing her. And yet—well, I wish I knew just what to do."

"Clean out of my line," says I.

I expect it was the roses that set me mullin' the case over again. They was sent over for Vee a couple of days later— half a dozen great busters, like young cabbages, with stems a yard long. They come with the compliments of Mrs. Ben Tupper.

"I simply couldn't send them back," says Vee; "and yet—"

"I get you," says I. "But don't worry. Let the thing ride a while. I got an idea."

It wasn't anything staggerin'. It had just struck me that if Vee had to hand out any social smears she ought to do it on her own dope, and not accordin' to Mrs. Pemmy Foote's say-so. Which is why I begins pumpin' information out of anybody that came handy. Goin' into town next mornin', I tackled three or four on the 8:03 in an offhand way.

Oh, yes, the Ben Tuppers! Business of hunchin' the shoulders. No, they didn't belong to the Country Club, nor the Hunt Association, nor figure on the Library or Hospital boards, or anything else. In fact, they don't mingle much. Hadn't made the grade. Barred? We-e-ell, in a way, perhaps. Why? Oh, there was Mrs. Ben. Wasn't she enough? An ex-actress with two or three hubbys in the discard! Could she expect people to swallow that?

Only one gent, though, had anything definite to offer. He's a middle-aged sport that seems to make a specialty of wearin' checked suits and yellow gloves. He chuckles when I mentions Mrs. Tupper.

"Grand old girl, Clara Belle," says he.

"Eh?" says I. "Shoot the rest."

"Couldn't think of it, son," says he. "You're too young. But in my day Clara Belle Kinney was some queen."

And that's all I can get out of him except more chuckles. I files away the name, though; and that afternoon, while we was waitin' for a quorum of directors to straggle into the General Offices, I springs it on Old Hickory.

"Mr. Ellins," says I, "did you ever know of a Clara Belle Kinney?"

"Wha-a-at?" he gasps, almost swallowin' his cigar. "Listen to that, Mason. Here's a young innocent asking if we ever knew Clara Belle Kinney. Did we?"

And old K. W. Mason, what does he do but throw back his shiny dome, open his mouth, and roar out:

"Yure right fut is crazy,
Yure left fut is lazy,
But if ye'll be aisy
I'll teach ye to waltz!"

After which them two old cut-ups wink at each other rakish and slap their knees. All of which ain't so illuminatin'. But they keep on, mentionin' Koster Bial's and the Cork Room, until I can patch together quite a sketch of Mrs. Tupper's early career.

Seems she'd made her first hit in this old-time concert-hall when she was a sweet young thing in her teens. One of her naughty stunts was kickin' her slipper into an upper box, and gettin' it tossed back with a mash note in it, or maybe a twenty-dollar bill. Then she'd graduated into comic opera.

"Was there ever a Katishaw like her?" demands Old Hickory of K. W., who responds by hummin' husky:

"I dote upon a tiger
From the Congo or the Niger,
Especially when lashing of his tail."

And, while they don't go into details, I gathered that they'd been Clara Belle fans—had sent her orchids on openin' nights, and maybe had set up wine suppers for her and her friends. They knew about a couple of her matrimonial splurges. One was with her manager, of course; the next was a young broker whose fam'ly got him to break it off. After that they'd lost track of her.

"It seems to me," says Old Hickory, "that I heard she had married someone in Buffalo, or Rochester, and had quit the stage. A patent medicine chap, I think he was, who'd made a lot of money out of something or other. I wonder what has become of her?"

That was my cue, all right, but I passes it up. I wasn't talkin' just then; I was listenin'.

"Ah-h-h!" goes on Mr. Mason, foldin' his hands over his forward sponson and rollin' his eyes sentimental. "Dear Clara Belle! I say, Ellins, wouldn't you like to hear her sing that MacFadden song once more?"

"I'd give fifty dollars," says Old Hickory.

"I'd make it a hundred if she'd follow it with 'O Promise Me,'" says K. W. "What was her record—six hundred nights on Broadway, wasn't it?"

Say, they went on reminiscin' so long, it's a wonder the monthly meetin' ever got started at all. I might have forgot them hot-air bids of theirs, too, if it hadn't been for something Vee announces that night across the dinner-table.

Seems that Mrs. Robert Ellins had been rung into managin' one of these war benefit stunts, and she's decided to use their new east terrace for an outdoor stage and the big drawin'-room it opens off from as an auditorium. You know, Mrs. Robert used to give violin recitals and do concert work herself, so she ain't satisfied with amateur talent. Besides, she knows so many professional people.

"And who do you think she is to have on the program?"

demands Vee. "Farrar!"

"Aw, come!" says I.

"And perhaps Mischa Elman," adds Vee. "Isn't that thrilling?"

I admits that it is.

"But say," I goes on, "with them big names on the bill, what does she expect to tax people for the best seats?"

Vee says how they'd figured they might ask ten dollars for a few choice chairs.

"Huh!" says I. "That won't get you far. Why don't you soak 'em proper?"

"But how?" asks Vee.

"You put in a bald-headed row," says I, "and I'll find you a party who'll fill it at a hundred a throw."

Vee stares at me like she thought I'd been touched with the heat, and wants to know who.

"Clara Belle Kinney," says I.

"Why, I never heard of any such person," says she.

"Oh, yes, you have," says I. "Alias Mrs. Ben Tupper."

Course, I had some job convincin' her I wasn't joshin'; and even after I'd sketched out the whole story, and showed her that Clara Belle's past wasn't anything to really shudder over, Vee is still doubtful.

"But can she sing now?" she asks.

"What's the odds," says I, "if a lot of them old-timers are willin' to pay to hear her try?"

Vee shakes her head and suggests that we go up and talk it over with Mr. and Mrs. Robert. Which we does.

"But if she has been off the stage for twenty years," suggests Mrs. Robert, "perhaps she wouldn't attempt it."

"I'll bet she would for Vee," says I. "Any way, she wouldn't feel sore at being asked And if you could sting a bunch of twenty or thirty for a hundred apiece—"

"Just fancy!" says Mrs. Robert, drawin' in a long breath and doin' rapid-fire mental arithmetic. "Verona, let's drive right over and see her at once."

They're some hustlers, that pair. All I have to do is map out the scheme, and they goes after it with a rush.

And say, I want to tell you that was a perfectly good charity concert, judged by the box-office receipts or any way you want to size it up. Bein' the official press-agent, who's got a better right to admit it?

True, Elman didn't show up, but his alibi was sound. And not until the last minute was we sure whether the fair Geraldine would get there or not. But my contribution to the headliners was there from the first tap of the bell.

Vee says she actually wept on her shoulder when the proposition was sprung on her. Seems she'd been livin' in Harbor Hills for nearly three years without havin' been let in on a thing—with nobody callin' on her, or even noddin' as she drove by. Most of her neighbors was a lot younger, folks who barely remembered that there had been such a party as Clara Belle Kinney, and who couldn't have told whether she'd been a singer or a bareback rider. They only knew her as a dumpy freakish dressed old girl whose drugged hair was turnin' gray.

"Of course," she says, sort of timid and trembly, "I have kept up my singing as well as I could. Mr. Tupper likes to have me. But I know my voice isn't what it was once. It's dear of you to ask me, though, and—and I'll do my best."

I don't take any credit for fillin' that double row of wicker chairs we put down front and had the nerve to ask that hold-up price for. When the word was passed around that Clara Belle Kinney was to be among the performers, they almost mobbed me for tickets. Why, I collected from two-thirds of the Corrugated directors without turnin' a hand, and for two days there about all I did was answer 'phone calls from Broad Street and the clubs—brokers, bank presidents, and so on, who wanted to know if there was any left.

A fine bunch of silver-tops they was, too, when we got 'em all lined up. You wouldn't have suspected it of some of them dignified old scouts, either. Back of 'em, fillin' every corner of the long room and spillin' out into the big hall, was the top crust of our local smart set, come to hear Farrar at close range.

Yep, Geraldine made quite a hit. Nothing strange about that. And that piece from "Madame Butterfly" she gave just brought 'em right up on their toes. But say, you should hear what breaks loose when it's announced that the third number will be an old favorite revival by Clara Belle Kinney. That's all the name we gave. What if most of the audience was simply starin' puzzled and stretchin' their necks to see who was comin'? Them old boys down front seemed to know what they was howlin' about.

Yes, Clara Belle does show up a bit husky in evenin' dress. Talk about elbow dimples! And I was wishin' she'd forgot to do her hair that antique way, all piled up on her head, with a few coy ringlets over one ear. But she'd landscaped her facial scenery artistic, and she sure does know how to roll them big eyes of hers.

I didn't much enjoy listenin' through them first few bars, though. There wasn't merely a crack here and there. Her voice went to a complete smash at times, besides bein' weak and wabbly. It's like listenin' to the ghost of a voice. I heard a few titters from the back rows.

But them old boys don't seem to mind. It was a voice comin' to them from 'way back in the '90's. And when she struggles through the first verse of "O Promise Me," and pauses to get her second wind, maybe they don't give her a hand. That seemed to pep her up a lot. She gets a better grip on the high notes, the tremolo effect wears off, and she goes to it like a winner. Begins to get the crowd with her, too. Why, say, even Farrar stands up and leads in the call for an encore. She ain't alone.

"MacFadden! MacFadden!" K. W. Mason is shoutin'.

So in a minute more Clara Belle, her eyes shinin', has swung into that raggy old tune, and when she gets to the chorus she beckons to the front rows and says: "Now, all together, boys!

"Wan—two—three!
Balance like me—"

Did they come in on it? Say, they roared it out like so many young college hicks riotin' around the campus after a session at a rathskeller. You should have seen Old Hickory standin' out front with his arms wavin' and his face red.

Then they demands some of the Katishaw stuff, and "Comrades," and "Little Annie Rooney." And with every encore Clara Belle seems to shake off five or ten years, until you could almost see what a footlight charmer she must have been.

In the midst of it all Vee gives me the nudge.

"Do look at Mr. Tupper, will you!"

Yes, he's sittin' over in a corner, with his white shirt-front bulgin', his neck stretched forward eager, and his big hairy paws grippin' the chair-back in front. And hanged if a drop of brine ain't tricklin' down one side of his nose.

"Gosh!" says I. "His emotions are leakin' into his whiskers. Maybe the old boy is human, after all."

A minute later, as I slides easy out of my end seat, Vee asks:

"Where are you going, Torchy?"

"I want a glimpse of Mrs. Pemmy Foote's face, that's all," says I.

CHAPTER VIII

WHEN TORCHY GOT THE CALL

No, I ain't said much about it before. There are some things you're apt to keep to yourself, specially the ones that root deep. And I'll admit that at first there I don't quite know where I was at. But as affairs got messier and messier, and the U-boats got busier, and I heard some first-hand details of what had happened to the Belgians—well, I got mighty restless. I expect I indulged in more serious thought stuff than I'd ever been guilty of.

You see, it was along back when we were gettin' our first close-ups of the big scrap—some of our boats sunk, slinkers reported off Sandy Hook, bomb plots shown up, and Papa Joffre over here soundin' the S. O. S. earnest.

Then there was Mr. Robert joinin' the Naval Reserves, and two young hicks from the bond room who'd volunteered. We'd had postals from 'em at the trainin' camp. Even Vee was busy with a first-aid class, learnin' how to tie bandages and put on splints.

So private seccing seemed sort of tame and useless—like keepin' on sprinklin' the lawn after your chimney was bein' struck by lightnin'. I felt like I ought to be gettin' in the game somehow. Anyway, it seemed as if it was my ante.

Not that I'd been rushed off my feet by all this buntin'-wavin' or khaki-wearin'. I'm no panicky Old Glory trail-hitter. Nor I didn't lug around the idea I was the missin' hero who was to romp through the barbed wire, stamp Hindenburg's whiskers in the mud, and lead the Allies across the Rhine. I didn't even kid myself I could swim out and kick a hole in a submarine, or do the darin' aviator act after a half-hour lesson at Mineola.

In fact, I suspected that sheddin' the enemy's gore wasn't much in my line. I knew I should dislike quittin' the hay at dawn to sneak out and get mixed up with half a bushel of impetuous scrap-iron. Still, if it had to be done, why not me as well as the next party?

I'd been meanin' to talk it over with Vee—sort of hint around, anyway, and see how she'd take it. But as a matter of fact I never could seem to find just the right openin' until, there one night after dinner, as she finishes a new piece she's tryin' over on the piano, I wanders up beside her and starts absent-minded tearin' little bits off a corner of the music.

"Torchy!" she protests. "What an absurd thing to do."

"Eh?" says I, twistin' it into a cornucopia. "But you know I can't go on warmin' the bench like this."

She stares at me puzzled for a second.

"Meaning what, for instance?" she asks.

"I got to go help swat the Hun," says I.

The flickery look in them gray eyes of hers steadies down,

and she reaches out for one of my hands. That's all. No jumpy emotions—not even a lip quiver.

"Must you?" says she, quiet.

"I can't take it out in wearin' a button or hirin' someone to hoe potatoes in the back lot," says I.

"No," says she.

"Auntie would come, I suppose?" says I.

Vee nods.

"And with Leon here," I goes on, "and Mrs. Battou, you could—"

"Yes, I could get along," she breaks in. "But—but when?"

"Right away," says I. "As soon as they can use me."

"You'll start training for a commission, then?" she asks.

"Not me," says I. "I'd be poor enough as a private, but maybe I'd help fill in one of the back rows. I don't know much about it. I'll look it up to-morrow."

"To-morrow? Oh!" says Vee, with just the suspicion of a break in her voice.

And that's all we had to say about it. Every word. You'd thought we'd exhausted the subject, or got the tongue cramp. But I expect we each had a lot of thoughts that didn't get registered. I know I did. And next mornin' the breakaway came sort of hard.

"I—I know just how you feel about it," says Vee.

"I'm glad somebody does, then," says I.

Puttin' the proposition up to Old Hickory was different. He shoots a quick glance at me from under them shaggy eyebrows, bites into his cigar savage, and grunts discontented.

"You are exempt, you know," says he.

"I know," says I. "If tags came with marriage licenses I might wear one on my watch-fob to show, I expect."

"Huh!" says he. "It seems to me that rapid-fire brain of yours might be better utilized than by hiding it under a trench helmet."

"Speedy thinkers seem to be a drug on the market just now," says I. "Anyway, I feel like it was up to me to deliver something—I can't say just what. But campin' behind a roll-top here on the nineteenth floor ain't going to help much, is it?"

"Oh, well, if you have the fever!" says he.

And half an hour later I've pushed in past the flag and am answerin' questions while the sergeant fills out the blank.

Maybe you can guess I ain't in any frivolous mood. I don't believe I thought I was about to push back the invader, or turn the tide for civilization. Neither was I lookin' on this as a sportin' flier or a larky excursion that I was goin' to indulge in at public expense. My idea was that there'd been a general call for such as me, and that I was comin' across. I was more or less sober about it.

They didn't seem much impressed at the recruitin' station.

Course, you couldn't expect the sergeant to get thrilled over every party that drifted in. He'd been there for weeks, I suppose, answerin' the same fool questions over and over, knowin' all the time that half of them that came in was bluffin' and that a big per cent. of the others wouldn't do.

But this other party with the zippy waistline, the swellin' chest, and the nifty shoulder-straps—why should he glare at me in that cold, suspicious way? I wasn't tryin' to break into the army with felonious intent. How could he be sure, just from a casual glance, that I was such vicious scum?

Oh, yes; I've figured out since that he didn't mean more'n half of it, or couldn't help lookin' at civilians that way after four years at West Point, or thought he had to. But that's what I get handed to me when I've dropped all the little things that seemed important to me and walks in to chuck what I had to offer Uncle Sam on the recruitin' table.

Some kind of inspectin' officer, I've found out he was, makin' the rounds to see that the sergeants didn't loaf on the job. And, just to show that no young patriot in a last year's Panama and a sport-cut suit could slip anything over on him, he shoots in a few crisp questions on his own account.

"Married, you say?" says he. "Since when?"

"Oh, this century," says I. "Last February, to get it nearer."

He sniffs disagreeable without sayin' why. Also he takes a hand when it comes to testin' me to see whether I'm club-footed or spavined. Course, I'm no perfect male like you see in the knit underwear ads, but I've got the usual number of toes and teeth, my wind is fairly good, and I don't expect my arteries have begun to harden yet. He listens to my heart action and measures my chest expansion. Then I had to name the different colors and squint through a tube at some black dots on a card.

And the further we went the more he scowled. Finally he shakes his head at the sergeant.

"Rejected," says he.

"Eh?" says I. "You—you don't mean I'm—turned down?"

He nods. "Underweight, and your eyes don't focus," says he snappy. "Here's your card. That's all."

Yes, it was a jolt. I expect I stood there blinkin' stupid at him for a minute or so before I had sense enough to drift out on the sidewalk. And I might as well admit I was feelin' mighty low. I didn't know whether to hunt up the nearest hospital, or sit down on the curb and wait until they came after me with the stretcher-cart. Anyway, I knew I must be a physical wreck. And to think I hadn't suspected it before!

Somehow I dragged back to the office, and a while later Mr. Ellins discovers me slumped in my chair with my chin down.

"Mars and Mercury!" says he. "You haven't been through a battle so soon, have you?"

At that, I tries to brace up a bit and pass it off light.

"Why didn't someone tell me I was a chronic invalid?" says I, after sketchin' out how my entry had been scratched by the chesty one. "I wonder where I could get a pair of crutches and a light-runnin' wheel chair?"

"Bah!" says he. "Some of those army officers have red-tape brains and no more common sense than he guinea-pigs.

What in the name of the Seven Shahs did he think was the matter with you?"

"My eyes don't track and I weigh under the scale," says I. "I expect there's other things, too. Maybe my floatin' ribs are water-logged and my memory muscle-bound. But I'm a wreck, all right."

"We'll see about that," says Old Hickory, pushin' a buzzer.

And inside of an hour I felt a lot better. I'd been gone over by a life insurance expert, who said I hadn't a soft spot on me, and an eye specialist had reported that my sight was up to the average. Oh, the right lamp did range a little further, but he claims that's often the case.

"Maybe my hair was too vivid for trench work," says I, "or else that captain was luggin' a grouch. Makes me feel like a wooden nickel at the bottom of the till, just the same; for I did hope I might be useful somehow. I'll look swell joinin' the home guards, won't I?"

"Don't overlook the fact, young man," puts in Old Hickory, "that the Corrugated Trust is not altogether out of this affair, and that we are running short-handed as it is."

I was too sore in my mind to be soothed much by that thought just then, though I did buckle into the work harder than ever.

As for Vee, she don't have much to say, but she gives me the close tackle when she hears the news.

"I don't care!" says she. "It was splendid of you to want to go. And I shall be just as proud of you as though you had been accepted."

"Oh, sure!" says I. "Likely I'll be mentioned in despatches for the noble way I handled the correspondence all through a hot spell."

That state of mind I didn't shake loose in a hurry, either. For three or four weeks, there, I was about the meekest commuter carried on the eight-three. I didn't do any gloatin' over the war news. I didn't join any of the volunteer boards of strategy that met every mornin' to tell each other how the subs ought to be suppressed, or what Haig should be doin' on the West front. I even stopped wearin' an enameled flag in my buttonhole. If that was all I could do, I wouldn't fourflush.

The Corrugated was handlin' a lot of war contracts, too. Course, we was only gettin' our ten per cent., and from some we'd subbed out not even that. It didn't strike me there was any openin' for me until I'd heard Mr. Ellins, for about the fourth time that week, start beefin' about the kind of work we was gettin' done.

"But ain't it all O. K.'d by government inspectors?" I asks.

"Precisely why I am suspicious," says he. "Not three per cent. turned back! And on rush work that's too good to be true. Looks to me like careless inspecting—or worse. Yet every man I've sent out has brought in a clean bill; even for the Wonder Motors people, who have that sub-contract for five hundred tanks. And I wouldn't trust that crowd to pass the hat for an orphans' home. I wish I knew of a man who could—could—By the Great Isosceles! Torchy!"

I knew I was elected when he first begun squintin' at me that way. But I couldn't see where I'd be such a wonderful find.

"A hot lot I know about buildin' armored motor-trucks, Mr.

Ellins," says I. "They could feed me anything."

"You let 'em," says he; "and meanwhile you unlimber that high-tension intellect of yours and see what you can pick up. Remember, I shall expect results from you, young man. When can you start for Cleveland? To-night, eh? Good! And just note this: It isn't merely the Corrugated Trust you are representing: it's Uncle Sam and the Allies generally. And if anything shoddy is being passed, you hunt it out. Understand?"

Yep. I did. And I'll admit I was some thrilled with the idea. But I felt like a Boy Scout being sent to round up a gang of gunfighters. I skips home, though, packs my bag, and climbs aboard the night express.

When I'd finally located the Wonder works, and had my credentials read by everyone, from the rookie sentry at the gate to the Assistant General Manager, and they was convinced I'd come direct from Old Hickory Ellins, they starts passin' out the smooth stuff. Oh, yes! Certainly! Anything special I wished to see?

"Thanks," says I. "I'll go right through."

"But we have four acres of shops, you know," suggests the A. G. M., smilin' indulgent.

"Maybe I can do an acre a day," says I. "I got lots of time."

"That's the spirit," says he, clappin' me friendly on the shoulder. "Walter, call in Mr. Marvin."

He was some grand little demonstrator, Mr. Marvin—one of these round-faced, pink-cheeked, chunky built young gents, who was as chummy and as entertainin' from the first handshake as if we'd been room-mates at college. I can't say how well posted he was on what was goin' on in the different departments he hustled me through, but he knew enough to smother me with machinery details.

"Now, here we have a battery of six hogging machines," he'd say. "They cut the gears, you know."

"Oh, yes," I'd say, tryin' to look wise.

It was that way all through the trip. I saw two or three thousand sweaty men in smeared overalls and sleeveless undershirts putterin' around lathes and things that whittled shavings off shiny steel bars, or hammered red-hot chunks of it into different shapes, or bit holes in great sheets of steel. I watched electric cranes the size of trolley cars juggle chunks of metal that weighed tons. I listened to the roar and rattle and crash and bang, and at the end of two hours my head was whirlin' as fast as some of them big belt wheels; and I knew almost as much about what I'd seen as a two-year-old does about the tick-tock daddy holds up to her ear.

Young Mr. Marvin don't seem discouraged, though. He suggests that we drive into town for lunch. We did, in a canary-colored roadster that purred along at about fifty most of the way. We fed at a swell club, along with a bunch of cheerful young lieutenants of industry who didn't seem worried about the high cost of anything. I gathered that most of 'em was in the same line as Mr. Marvin—supplies or munitions. From the general talk, and the casual way they ordered pink cocktails and expensive cigars, I judged it wasn't exactly a losin' game.

Nor they didn't seem anxious about gettin' back to punch in on the time-clocks. About two-thirty we adjourns to the Country Club, and if I'd been a mashie fiend I might have finished a hard day's work with a game of golf. I thought I ought to do some more shops, though. Why, to be sure! But at five we knocked off again, and I was towed to another club, where we had a plunge in a marble pool so as to be in shape for a little dinner Mr. Marvin was gettin' up for me. Quite some dinner! There was a jolly trip out to an amusement park later on. Oh, the Wonder folks were no tightwads when it came to showin' special agents of the Corrugated around.

I tried another day of it before givin' up. It was no use. They had me buffaloed. So I thanked all hands and hinted that maybe I'd better be goin' back. I hope I didn't deceive anyone, for I did go back—to the hotel. But by night I'd invested $11.45 in a second-hand outfit—warranted steam-cleaned—and I had put up $6. more for a week's board with a Swede lady whose front porch faced the ten-foot fence guardin' the Wondor Motors' main plant. Also, Mrs. Petersen had said it was a cinch I could get a job. Her old man would show me where in the mornin'.

And say, mornin' happens early out in places like that. By 5:30 A.M. I could smell bacon grease, and by six-fifteen breakfast was all over and Petersen had lit his corn-cob pipe.

"Coom!" says he in pure Scandinavian.

This trip, I didn't make my entrance in over the Turkish rugs of the private office. I was lined up with a couple of dozen others against a fence about tenth from a window where there was a "Men Wanted" sign out. Being about as much of a mechanic as I am a brunette, I made no wild bluffs. I just said I wanted a job. And I got it—riveter's helper, whatever that might be. By eight-thirty my name and number was on the payroll, and the foreman of shop No. 19 was introducin' me to my new boss.

"Here, Mike," says he. "Give this one a try-out."

His name wasn't Mike. It was something like Sneezowski.
He was a Pole who'd come over three years ago to work for
John D. at Bayonne, New Jersey, but had got into some kind
of trouble there. I didn't wonder. He had wicked little eyes,
one lopped ear, and a ragged mustache that stood out like
tushes. But he sure could handle a pneumatic riveter rapid,
and when it came to reprovin' me for not keepin' the pace he
expressed himself fluent.

In the course of a couple of hours, though, I got the hang of
how to work them rivet tongs without droppin' 'em more 'n
once every five minutes. But I think it was the grin I slipped
Mike now and then that got him to overlookin' my awkward
motions. Believe me, too, by six o'clock I felt less like
grinnin' than any time I could remember. I never knew you
could ache in so many places at once. From the ankles down
I felt fine. And yet, before the week was out I was helpin'
Mike speed up.

It didn't look promisin' for sleuth work at first. Half a dozen
times I was on the point of chuckin' the job. But the thoughts
of havin' to face Old Hickory with a blank report kept me
pluggin' away. I begun to get my bearin's a bit to see things,
to put this and that together.

We was workin' on shaped steel plates, armor for the tanks.
Now and then one would come through with some of the
holes only quarter or half punched. Course, you couldn't put
rivets in them places.

"How about these?" I asks.

"Aw, wottell!" says Mike. "Forget it."

"But what if the inspector sees?" I insists.

Mike gurgles in his throat, indicatin' mirth.

"Th' inspec'!" he chuckles. "Him wink by his eye, him. Ya! You see! Him coom Sat'day."

And I swaps chuckles with Mike. Also, by settin' up the schooners at Carlouva's that evenin', I got Mike to let out more professional secrets along the same line. There was others who joined in. They bragged of chipped gears that was shipped through with the bad cogs covered with grease, of flawy drivin' shafts, of cheesy armor-plate that you could puncture with a tack-hammer.

While it was all fresh that night I jotted down pages of such gossip in a little red note-book. I had names and dates. That bunch of piece-workers must have thought I was a bear for details, or else nutty in the head; but they was too polite to mention it so long as I insisted each time that it was my buy.

Anyway, I got quite a lot of first-hand evidence as to the kind of inspectin' done by the army officer assigned to this particular plant. I had to smile, too, when I saw Mr. Marvin towin' him through our shop Saturday forenoon. Maybe they was three minutes breezin' through. And I didn't need the extra smear of smut on my face. Marvin never glanced my way. This was the same officer who'd been in on our dinner party, too.

Yes, I found chattin' with Mike and his friends a lot more illuminatin' than listenin' to Mr. Marvin. So, when I drew down my second pay envelop, I told the clerk I was quittin'. I don't mind sayin', either, that it seemed good to splash around in a reg'lar bath-tub once more and to look a sirloin steak in the face again. A stiff collar did seem odd, though.

Me and Mr. Ellins had some session. We went through that red note-book thorough. He was breathin' a bit heavy at times, and he chewed hard on his cigar all the way; but he never blew a fuse until forty-eight hours later. The General Manager of Wonder Motors, four department heads, and the army officer detailed as inspector was part of the audience. They'd been called on the carpet by wire, and was grouped around one end of our directors' table. At the other end was Old Hickory, Mr. Robert, Piddie, and me.

Item by item, Mr. Ellins had sketched out to the Wonder crowd the bunk stuff they'd been slippin' over. First they tried protestin' indignant; then they made a stab at actin' hurt; but in the end they just looked plain foolish.

"My dear Mr. Ellins," put in the General Manager, "one cannot watch every workman in a plant of that magnitude. Besides," here he hunches his shoulders, "if the government is satisfied—"

"Hah!" snorts Old Hickory. "But it isn't. For I'm the government in this instance. I'm standing for Uncle Sam. That's what I meant when I took those ten per cent. contracts. I'm too old to go out and fight his enemies abroad, but I can stay behind and watch for yellow-livered buzzards such as you. Call that business, do you? Fattening your dividends by sending our boys up against the Prussian guns in junky motor-tanks covered with tin armor! Bah! Your ethics need chloride of lime on them. And you come here whining that you can't watch your men! By the great sizzling sisters, we'll see if you can't! You will put in every missing rivet, replace every flawy plate, and make every machine perfect, or I'll smash your little two-by-four concern so flat the bankruptcy courts won't find enough to tack a libel notice on. Now go back and get busy."

They seemed in a hurry to start, too.

An hour or so later, when Old Hickory had stopped steaming, he passes out a different set of remarks to me. Oh, the usual grateful boss stuff. Even says he's going to make the War Department give me a commission, with a special detail.

"Wouldn't that be wonderful!" says Vee, clappin' her hands. "Do you really think he will? A lieutenant, perhaps?"

"That's what he mentioned," says I.

"Really!" says Vee, makin' a rush at me.

"Wait up!" says I. "Halt, I mean. Now, as you were! Salute!"

"Pooh!" says Vee, continuin' her rush.

But say, she knows how to salute, all right. Her way would break up an army, though. All the same, I guess I've earned it, for by Monday night I'll be up in a Syracuse shovel works, wearin' a one-piece business suit of the Never-rip brand, and I'll likely have enough grease on me to lubricate a switch-engine.

"It's lucky you don't see me, Vee," says I, "when I'm out savin' the country. You'd wonder how you ever come to do it."

CHAPTER IX

A CARRY-ON FOR CLARA

"Now turn around," says Vee. "Oh, Torchy! Why, you look perfectly—"

"Do I?" I cuts in. "Well, you don't think I'm goin' to the office like this, do you?"

She does. Insists that Mr. Ellins will expect it.

"Besides," says she, "it is in the army regulations that you must. If you don't—well, I'm not sure whether it is treason or mutiny."

"Hal-lup!" says I. "I surrender."

So I starts for town lookin' as warlike as if I'd just come from a front trench, and feelin' like a masquerader who'd lost his way to the ball-room.

In the office, Old Hickory gives me the thorough up-and-down. It's a genial, fatherly sort of inspection, and he ends it with a satisfied grunt.

"Good-morning, Lieutenant," says he. "I see you have—er—

got 'em on. And, allow me to mention, rather a good fit, sir."

I gasps. Sirred by Old Hickory! Do you wonder I got fussed? But he only chuckles easy, waves me to take a chair, and goes on with:

"What's the word from the Syracuse sector?"

At that, I gets my breath back.

"Fairly good deal up there, sir," says I. "They're workin' in a carload or so of wormy ash for the shovel handles, and some of the steel runs below test; but most of their stuff grades well. I'll have my notes typed off right away."

After I've filed my report I should have ducked. But this habit of stickin' around the shop is hard to break. And that's how I happen to be on hand when the lady in gray drifts in for her chatty confab with Mr. Ellins.

Seems she held quite a block of our preferred, for when Vincent lugs in her card Old Hickory spots the name right away as being on our widow-and-orphan list that we wave at investigatin' committees.

"Ah, yes!" says he. "Mrs. Parker Smith. Show her in, boy."

Such a quiet, gentle, dignified party she is, her costume tonin' in with her gray hair, and an easy way of speakin' and all, that my first guess is she might be the head of an old ladies' home.

"Mr. Ellins," says she, "I am looking for my niece."

"Are you?" says Mr. Ellins, "Humph! Hardly think we could be of service in such a case."

"Oh!" says she. "I—I am so sorry."

"Lost, is she?" suggests Mr. Ellins, weakenin'.

"She is somewhere in New York," goes on Mrs. Parker Smith. "Of course, I know it is an imposition to trouble you with such a matter. But I thought you might have someone in your office who—who—"

"We have," says he. "Torchy,—er—I mean, Lieutenant,—Mrs. Parker Smith. Here, madam, is a young man who will find your niece for you at once. In private life he is my secretary; and as it happens that just now he is on special detail, his services are entirely at your disposal."

She looks a little doubtful about bein' shunted like that, but she follows me into the next room, where I produces a pencil and pad and calls for details businesslike.

"Let's see," says I. "What's the full description? Age?"

"Why," says she, hesitatin', "Claire is about twenty-two."

"Oh!" says I. "Got beyond the flapper stage, then. Height—tall or short?"

Mrs. Parker Smith shakes her head.

"I'm sure I don't know," says she. "You see, Claire is not an own niece. She—well, she is a daughter of my first husband's second wife's step-sister."

"Wha-a-at?" says I, gawpin' at her. "Daughter of your—Oh, say, let's not go into it as deep as that. I'm dizzy already. Suppose we call her an in-law once removed and let it go at that?"

"Thank you," says Mrs. Parker Smith, givin' me a quizzin' smile. "Perhaps it is enough to say that I have never seen her."

She does go on to explain, though, that when Claire's step-uncle, or whatever he was, found his heart trouble gettin' worse, he wrote to Mrs. Parker Smith, askin' her to forget the past and look after the orphan girl that he's been tryin' to bring up. It's just as clear to me as the average movie plot, but I nods my head.

"So for three years," says she, "while Claire was in boarding-school, I acted as her guardian; but since she has come of age I have been merely the executor of her small estate."

"Oh, yes!" says I. "And now she's come to New York, and forgot to send you her address?"

It was something like that. Claire had gone in for art. Looked like she'd splurged heavy on it, too; for the drain on her income had been something fierce. Meanwhile, Mrs. Parker Smith had doped out an entirely different future for Claire. The funds that had been tied up in a Vermont barrel-stave fact'ry, that was makin' less and less barrel staves every year, Auntie had pulled out and invested in a model dairy farm out near Rockford, Illinois. She'd made the capital turn over from fifteen to twenty per cent., too, by livin' right on the job and cashin' in the cream tickets herself.

"You have!" says I. "Not a reg'lar cow farm?"

She nods.

"It did seem rather odd, at first," says she. "But I wanted to get away from—from everything. But now—Well, I want Claire. I suppose I am a little lonesome. Besides, I want her to try taking charge. Recently, when she had drawn her income for half a year in advance and still asked for more, I was obliged to refuse."

"And then?" says I.

Mrs. Parker Smith shrugs her shoulders.

"The foolish girl chose to quarrel with me," says she. "About ten days ago she sent me a curt note. I could keep her money; she was tired of being dictated to. I needn't write any more, for she had moved to another address, had changed her name."

"Huh!" says I. "That does make it complicated. You don't know what she looks like, or what name she flags under, and I'm to find her in little New York?"

But I finds myself tacklin this hopeless puzzle from every angle I could think of. I tried 'phonin' to Claire's old street number. Nothin' doin'. They didn't know anything about Miss Hunt.

"What brand of art was she monkeyin' with?" I asks.

Mrs. Parker Smith couldn't say. Claire hadn't been very chatty in her letters. Chiefly she had demanded checks.

"But in one she did mention," says the lady in gray, "that— Now, what was it! Oh, yes! Something about 'landing a cover.' What could that mean?"

"Cover?" says I. "Why, for a magazine, maybe. That's it. And if we only knew what name she'd sign, we might— Would she stick to the Claire part? I'll bet she would. Wait. I'll get a bunch of back numbers from the arcade news-stand

and we'll go through 'em."

We'd hunted through an armful, though, before we runs across this freaky sketch of a purple nymph, with bright yellow hair, bouncin' across a stretch of dark blue lawn.

"Claire Lamar!" says I. "Would that be—Eh? What's wrong?"

Mrs. Parker Smith seems to be gettin' a jolt of some kind, but she steadies herself and almost gets back her smile.

"I—I am sure it would," says she. "It's very odd, though."

"Oh, I don't know," says I. "Listens kind of arty—Claire Lamar. Lemme see. This snappy fifteen-center has editorial offices on Fourth Avenue and—Well, well! Barry Frost, ad. manager! Say, if I can get him on the wire—"

Just by luck, I did. Would he pry some facts for me out of the art editor, facts about a certain party? Sure he would. And inside of ten minutes, without leavin' the Corrugated General Offices, I had a full description of Claire, includin' where she hung out.

"Huh!" says I. "Greenwich Village, eh? You might know."

"My dear Lieutenant," says Mrs. Parker Smith, "I think you are perfectly wonderful."

"Swell thought!" says I. "But you needn't let on to Mr. Ellins how simple it was. And now, all you got to do is—"

"I know," she cuts in. "And I really ought not to trouble you another moment. But, since Mr. Ellins has been so kind— well, I am going to ask you to help me just a trifle more."

"Shoot," says I, unsuspicious.

It ain't much, she says. But she's afraid, if she trails Claire to her rooms, the young lady might send down word she was out, or make a quick exit.

"But if you would go," she suggests, "with a note from me asking her to join us somewhere at dinner—"

I holds up both hands.

"Sorry," says I, "but I got to duck. That's taking too many chances."

Then I explains how, although I may look like a singleton, I'm really the other half of a very interestin' domestic sketch, and that Vee's expectin' me home to dinner.

"Why, all the better!" says Mrs. Parker Smith. "Have her come in and join us. I'll tell you: we will have our little party down at the old Napoleon, where they have such delicious French cooking. Now, please."

As I've hinted before, she is some persuader. I ain't mesmerized so strong, though, but what I got sense enough to play it safe by callin' up Vee first. I don't think she was strong for joinin' the reunion until I points out that I might be some shy at wanderin' down into the art-student colony and collectin' a strange young lady illustrator all by myself.

"Course, I could do it alone if I had to," I throws in.

"H-m-m-m!" says Vee. "If that bashfulness of yours is likely to be as bad as all that, perhaps I'd better come."

So by six o 'clock Vee and I are in the dinky reception-room of one of them Belasco boardin'-houses, tryin' to convince a young female in a paint-splashed smock and a floppy boudoir cap that we ain't tryin' to kidnap or otherwise annoy her.

"What's the big idea?" says she. "I don't get you at all."

"Maybe if you'd read the note it would help," I suggests.

"Oh!" says she, and takes it over by the window.

She's a long-waisted, rangy young party, who walks with a Theda Bara slouch and tries to talk out of one side of her mouth. "Hello!" she goes on. "The Parker Smith person. That's enough. It's all off."

"Just as you say," says I. "But, if you ask me, I wouldn't pass up an aunt like her without takin' a look."

"Aunt!" says Claire Lamar, *alias* Hunt. "Listen: she's about as much an aunt to me as I am to either of you. And I've never shed any tears over the fact, either. The only aunt that I'd ever own was one that my family would never tell me much about. I had to find out about her for myself. Take it from me, though, she was some aunt."

"Tastes in aunts differ, I expect," says I. "And Mrs. Parker Smith don't claim to be a reg'lar aunt, anyway. She seems harmless, too. All she wants is a chance to give you a rosy prospectus of life on a cow farm and blow you to a dinner at the Napoleon."

"Think of that!" says Claire. "And I've been living for weeks on window-sill meals, with now and then a ptomaine-defying gorge at the Pink Poodle's sixty-cent table d'hote. Oh, I'll come, I'll come! But I warn you: the Parker Smith person will understand before the evening is over that I was born to no cow farm in Illinois."

With that she glides off to do a dinner change.

"I believe it is going to be quite an interesting party, don't you?" says Vee.

"The signs point that way," says I. "But the old girl really ought to wear shock-absorbers if she wants to last through the evenin'. S-s-s-sh! Claire is comin' back."

This time she's draped herself in a pale yellow kimono with blue triangles stenciled all over it.

"Speaking of perfectly good aunts," says she, "there!" And she displays a silver-framed photo. It's an old-timer done in faded brown, and shows a dashin' young party wearin' funny sleeves, a ringlet cascade on one side of her head, and a saucy little pancake lid over one ear.

"That," explains Claire, "was my aunt Clara Lamar; not my real aunt, you know, but near enough for me to claim her. This was taken in '82, I believe."

"Really!" says Vee. "She must have been quite pretty."

"That doesn't half tell it," says Claire. "She was a charmer, simply fascinating. Not beautiful, you know, but she had a way with her. She was brilliant, daring, one of the kind that men raved over. At twenty she married a Congressman, fat and forty. She hadn't lived in Washington six months before her receptions were crushes. She flirted industriously. A young French aide and an army officer fought a duel over her. And, while the capital was buzzing with that, she eloped with another diplomat, a Russian. For a year or two they lived in Paris. She had her salon. Then the Russian got himself killed in some way, and she soon married again— another American, quite wealthy. He brought her back to New York, and they lived in one of those old brown-stone mansions on lower Fifth Avenue. Her dinner parties were the talk of the town—champagne with the fish, vodka with the coffee, cigarettes for the women, cut-up stunts afterwards. I forget just who No. 3 was, but he succumbed. Couldn't stand the pace, I suppose. And then—Well, Aunt Clara disappeared. But, say, she was a regular person. I wish I could find out what ever became of her."

"Maybe Mrs. Parker Smith could give you a line," I suggests.

"Her!" says Claire. "Fat chance! But I must finish dressing. Sorry to keep you waiting."

We did get a bit restless durin' the next half hour, but the wait was worth while. For, believe me, when Claire comes down again she's some dolled.

I don't mean she was any home-destroyer. That face of hers is too long and heavy for the front row of a song review. But she has plenty of zip to her get-up. After one glance I calls a taxi.

The way I'd left it with Mrs. Parker Smith, we was to land Claire at the hotel first; then call her up, and proceed to order dinner. So we had another little stage wait, with only the three of us at the table.

"I hope you don't mind if I have a puff or two," says Claire. "It goes here, you know."

"Anything to make the evenin' a success," says I, signalin' a garcon. "My khaki lets me out of followin' you."

So, when the head waiter finally tows in Mrs. Parker Smith, costumed in the same gray dress and lookin' meeker and gentler than ever, she is greeted with a sporty tableau. But she don't faint or anything. She just springs that twisty smile of hers and comes right on.

"The missing one!" says I, wavin' at Claire.

"Ah!" says Mrs. Parker Smith, beamin' on her. "So good of you to come!"

"Wasn't it?" says Claire, removin' the cork tip languid.

Well, as a get-together I must admit that the outlook was kind of frosty. Claire showed plenty of enthusiasm for the hors d'oeuvres and the low-tide soup and so on, but mighty little for this volunteer auntie, who starts to describe the subtle joys of the butter business.

"Perhaps you have never seen a herd of registered Guernseys," says Mrs. Parker Smith, "when they are munching contentedly at milking time, with their big, dreamy eyes—"

"Excuse me!" says Claire. "I don't have to. I spent a whole month's vacation on a Vermont farm."

Mrs. Parker Smith only smiles indulgent.

"We use electric milkers, you know," says she, "and most of our young men come from the agricultural colleges."

"That listens alluring—some," admits Claire. "But I can't see myself planted ten miles out on an R. F. D. route, even with college-bred help. Pardon me if I light another dope-stick."

I could get her idea easy enough, by then. Claire wasn't half so sporty as she hoped she was. It was just her way of doing the carry-on for Aunt Clara Lamar. But, at the same time, we couldn't help feelin' kind of sorry for Mrs. Parker Smith. She was tryin' to be so nice and friendly, and she wasn't gettin' anywhere.

It was by way of switchin' the line of table chat, I expect, that Vee breaks in with that remark about the only piece of jewelry the old girl is wearin'.

"What a duck of a bracelet!" says Vee. "An heirloom, is it?"

"Almost," says Mrs. Parker Smith. "It was given to me on my twenty-second birthday, in Florence."

She slips it off and passes it over for inspection. The part that goes around the wrist is all of fine chain-work, silver and gold, woven almost like cloth, and on top is a cameo, 'most as big as a clam.

"How stunning! Look, Torchy. O-o-oh!" says Vee, gaspin' a little.

In handling the thing she must have pressed a catch somewhere, for the cameo springs back, revealin' a locket effect underneath with a picture in it. Course, we couldn't help seein'.

"Why—why—" says Vee, gazin' from the picture to Mrs. Parker Smith. "Isn't this a portrait of—of—"

"Of a very silly young woman," cuts in Auntie. "We waited in Florence a week to have that finished."

"Then—then it is you!" asks Vee.

The lady in gray nods. Vee asks if she may show it to Claire.

"Why not?" says Mrs. Parker Smith, smilin'.

We didn't stop to explain. I passes it on to Claire, and then we both watches her face. For the dinky little picture under the cameo is a dead ringer for the one Claire had shown us in the silver frame. So it was Claire's turn to catch a short breath.

"Don't tell me," says she, "that—that you are Clara Lamar?"

Which was when Auntie got her big jolt. For a second the pink fades out of her cheeks, and the salad fork she'd been holdin' rattles into her plate. She makes a quick recovery, though.

"I was—once," says she. "I had hoped, though, that the name had been forgotten. Tell me, how—how do you happen to—"

"Why," says Claire, "uncle had the scrapbook habit. Anyway, I found this one in an old desk, and it was all about you. Your picture was in it, too. And say, Auntie, you were the real thing, weren't you?"

After that it was a reg'lar reunion. For Claire had dug up her heroine. And, no matter how strong Auntie protests that she ain't that sort of a party now, and hasn't been for years and years, Claire keeps right on. She's a consistent admirer, even if she is a little late.

"If I had only known it was you!" says she.

"Then—then you'll come to Meadowbrae with me?" asks Mrs. Parker Smith.

"You bet!" says Claire. "Between you and me, this art career of mine has rather fizzled out. Besides, keeping it up has got to be rather a bore. Honest, a spaghetti and cigarette life is a lot more romantic to read about than it is to follow. Whether I could learn to run a dairy farm or not, I don't know; but, with an aunt like you to coach me along, I'm blessed if I don't give it a try. When do we start?"

"But," says Vee to me, later, "I can't imagine her on a farm."

"Oh, I don't know," says I. "Didn't you notice she couldn't smoke without gettin' it up her nose?"

CHAPTER X

ALL THE WAY WITH ANNA

Believe me, Belinda, this havin' a boss who's apt to stack you up casual against stuff that would worry a secret service corps recruited from seventh sons is a grand little cure for monotonous moments. Just because I happen to get a few easy breaks on my first special details seems to give Old Hickory the merry idea that when he wants someone to do the wizard act, all he has to do is press the button for me. I don't know whether my wearin' the khaki uniform helps out the notion or not. I shouldn't wonder.

Now, here a week or ten days ago, when I leaves Vee and my peaceful little home after a week-end swing, I expects to be shot up to Amesbury, Mass., to inspect a gun-limber factory. Am I? Not at all. By 3 P.M. I'm in Bridgeport, Conn., wanderin' about sort of aimless, and tryin' to size up a proposition that I'm about as well qualified to handle as a plumber's helper called in to tune a pipe organ.

Why was it that some three thousand hands in one of our sub-contractin' plants was bent on gettin' stirred up and messy about every so often, in spite of all that had been done to soothe 'em?

Sewell Ford

Does that listen simple, or excitin', or even interestin'? It didn't to me. Specially after I'd given the once-over to this giddy mob of Wops and Hunkies and Sneezowskis.

The office people didn't know how many brands of Czechs or Magyars or Polacks they had in the shops. What they was real sure of was that a third of the bunch had walked out twice within the last month, and if they quit again, as there was signs of their doin', we stood to drop about $200,000 in bonuses on shell contracts.

It wasn't a matter of wage scales, either. Honest, some of them ginks with three z's in their names was runnin' up, with over-time and all, pay envelops that averaged as much as twelve a day. Why, some of the women and girls were pullin' down twenty-five a week. And they couldn't kick on the workin' conditions, either. Here was a brand-new concrete plant, clean as a new dish-pan, with half the sides swingin' glass sashes, and flower beds outside.

"And still they threaten another strike," says the general manager. "If it comes, we might as well scrap this whole plant and transfer the equipment to Pennsylvania or somewhere else. Unless"—here he grins sarcastic—"you can find out what ails 'em, Lieutenant. But you are only the third bright young man the Corrugated has sent out to tell us what's what, you know."

"Oh, well," says I. "There's luck in odd numbers. Cheer up."

It was after this little chat that I sheds the army costume and wanders out disguised as a horny-handed workingman.

Not that I'd decided to get a job right away. After my last stab I ain't so strong for this ten-hour cold-lunch trick as I was when I was new to the patriotic sleuthin' act. Besides, bein' no linguist, I couldn't see how workin' with such a mixed lot was goin' to get me anywhere. If I could only run across a good ambidextrous interpreter, now, one who could listen in ten languages and talk in six, it might help. And who was it I once knew that had moved to Bridgeport?

I'd been mullin' on that mystery ever since I struck the town. Just a glimmer, somewhere in the back of my nut, that there had been such a party some time or other. I'll admit that wasn't much of a clue to start out trailin' in a place of this size, but it's all I had.

I must have walked miles, readin' the signs on the stores, pushin' my way through the crowds, and finally droppin' into a fairly clean-lookin' restaurant for dinner. Half way through the goulash and noodles, I had this bright thought about consultin' the 'phone book. The cashier that let me have it eyed me suspicious as I props it up against the sugar bowl and starts in with the A's.

Ever try readin' a telephone directory straight through? By the time I'd got through the M's I'd had to order another cup of coffee and a second piece of lemon pie. At that, the waitress was gettin' uneasy. She'd just shoved my check at me for the third time, and was addin' a glass of wooden tooth-picks, when I lets out this excited stage whisper.

"Sobowski!" says I, grabbin' the book.

The young lady in the frilled apron rests her thumbs on her hips dignified and shoots me a haughty glance. "Ring off, young feller," says she. "You got the wrong number."

"Not so, Clarice," says I. "His first name is Anton, and he used to run a shine parlor in the arcade of the Corrugated buildin', New York, N. Y."

"It's a small world, ain't it?" says she. "You can pay me or at the desk, just as you like."

Clarice got her tip all right, and loaned me her pencil to write down Anton's street number.

A stocky, bow-legged son of Kosciuszko, built close to the ground, and with a neck on him like a truck-horse, as I remembered Anton. But the hottest kind of a sport. Used to run a pool on the ball-games, and made a book on the ponies now and then. Always had a roll with him. He'd take a nickel tip from me and then bet a guy in the next chair fifty to thirty-five the Giants would score more'n three runs against the Cubs' new pitcher in to-morrow's game. That kind.

Must have been two or three years back that Anton had told me about some openin' he had to go in with a brother-in-law up in Bridgeport. Likely I didn't pay much attention at the time. Anyway, he was missin' soon after; and if I hadn't been in the habit of callin' him Old Sobstuff I'd have forgotten that name of his entirely. But seein' it there in the book brought back the whole thing.

"Anton Sobowski, saloon," was the way it was listed. So he was runnin' a suds parlor, eh? Well, it wasn't likely he'd know much about labor troubles, but it wouldn't do any harm to look him up. When I came to trail down the street number, though, blamed if it ain't within half a block of our branch works.

And, sure enough, in a little office beyond the bar, leanin' back luxurious in a swivel-chair, and displayin' a pair of baby-blue armlets over his shirt sleeves, I discovers Mr. Sobowski himself. It ain't any brewery-staked hole-in-the-wall he's boss of, either. It's the Warsaw Cafe, bar and restaurant, all glittery and gorgeous, with lace curtains in the front windows, red, white, and blue mosquito nettin' draped artistic over the frosted mirrors, and three busy mixers behind the mahogany bar.

Anton has fleshed up considerable since he quit jugglin' the brushes, and he's lost a little of the good-natured twinkle from his wide-set eyes. He glances up at me sort of surly when I first steps into the office; but the minute I takes off the straw lid and ducks my head at him, he lets loose a rumbly chuckle.

"It is that Torchy, hey?" says he. "Well, well! It don't fade any, does it?"

"Not that kind of dye," says I. "How's the boy?"

"Me," says Anton. "Oh, fine like silk. How you like the place, hey?"

I enthused over the Warsaw Cafe; and when he found I was still with the Corrugated, and didn't want to touch him for any coin, but had just happened to be in town and thought I'd look him up for old times' sake—well, Anton opened up considerable.

"What!" says he. "They send you out? You must be comin' up?"

"Only private sec. to Mr. Ellins," says I, "but he chases me around a good deal. We're busy people these days, you know."

"The Corrugated Trust! I should say so," agrees Anton, waggin' his head earnest. "Big people, big money. I like to have my brother-in-law meet you. Wait."

Seemed a good deal like wastin' time, but I spent the whole evenin' with Anton. I met not only the brother-in-law, but also Mrs. Sobowski, his wife; and another Mrs. Sobowski, an aunt or something; and Miss Anna Sobowski, his niece. Also I saw the three-story Sobowski boardin'-house that Anton conducted on the side; and the Alcazar movie joint, another Sobowski enterprise.

That's where this Anna party was sellin' tickets—a peachy-cheeked, high-chested young lady with big, rollin' eyes, and her mud-colored hair waved something wonderful. I was introduced reg'lar and impressive.

"Anna," says Anton, "take a good look at this young man. He's a friend of mine. Any time he comes by, pass him in free—any time at all. See?"

And Anna, she flashes them high-powered eyes of hers at me kittenish. "Aw ri'," says she. "I'm on, Mr. Torchy."

"That girl," confides Anton to me afterwards, "was eating black bread and cabbage soup in Poland less than three years ago. Now she buys high kid boots, two kinds of leather, at fourteen dollars. And makes goo-goo eyes at all the men. Yes, but never no mistakes with the change. Not Anna."

All of which was interestin' enough, but it didn't seem to help any. You never can tell, though, can you? You see, it was kind of hard, breakin' away from Anton once he'd started to get folksy and show me what an important party he'd come to be. He wanted me to see the Warsaw when it was really doin' business, about ten o'clock, after the early picture-show crowds had let out and the meetin' in the hall overhead was in full swing.

"What sort of meetin'?" I asks, just as a filler.

"Oh, some kind of labor meetin'," says he. "I d'know. They chin a lot. That's thirsty work. Good for business, hey?"

"Is it a labor union?" I insists.

Anton shrugs his shoulders.

"You wait," says he. "Mr. Stukey, he'll tell you all about it. Yes, an ear-full. He's a good spender, Stukey. Hires the hall, too."

Somehow, that listened like it might be a lead. But an hour later, when I'd had a chance to look him over, I was for passin' Stukey up. For he sure was disappointin' to view. One of these thin, sallow, dyspeptic parties, with deep lines down either side of his mouth, a bristly, jutty little mustache, and ratty little eyes.

I expect Anton meant well when he brings out strong, in introducin' me, how I'm connected with the Corrugated Trust. In fact, you might almost gather I *was* the Corrugated. But it don't make any hit with Stukey.

"Hah!" says he, glarin' at me hostile. "A minion."

"Solid agate yourself," says I. "Wha'd'ye mean—minion?"

"Aren't you a hireling of the capitalistic class?" demands Stukey.

"Maybe," says I, "but I ain't above mixin' with lower-case minds now and then."

"Case?" says he. "I don't understand."

"Perhaps that's your trouble," says I.

"Bah!" says he, real peevish.

"Come, come, boys!" says Anton, clappin' us jovial on the shoulders. "What's this all about, hey? We are all friends here. Yes? Is it that the meetin' goes wrong, Mr. Stukey? Tell us, now."

Stukey shakes his head at him warnin'. "What meetin'?" says he. "Don't be foolish. What time is it? Ten-twenty! I have an engagement."

And with that he struts off important.

Anton hunches his shoulders and lets out a grunt.

"He has it bad—Stukey," says he. "It is that Anna. Every night he must walk home with her."

"She ain't particular, is she?" I suggests.

"Oh, I don't know," says Anton. "Yes, he is older, and not a strong hearty man, like some of these young fellows. But he is educated; oh, like the devil. You should hear him talk once."

But Stukey had stirred up a stubborn streak in me.

"Is he, though," says I, "or do you kid yourself?"

I thought that would get a come-back out of Anton. And it does.

"If I am so foolish," says he, "would I be here, with my name in gold above the door, or back shining shoes in the Corrugated arcade yet? Hey? I will tell you this. Nobodies don't come and hire my hall from me, fifty a week, in advance."

"Cash or checks?" I puts in.

"If the bank takes the checks, why should I worry?" asks Anton.

"Oh, the first one might be all right," says I, "and the second; but—well, you know your own business, I expect."

Anton gazes at me stupid for a minute, then turns to his desk and fishes out a bunch of returned checks. He goes through 'em rapid until he has run across the one he's lookin' for.

"Maybe I do," says he, wavin' it under my nose triumphant.

Which gives me the glimpse I'd been jockeyin' for. The name of that bank was enough. From then on I was mighty interested in this Mortimer J. Stukey; and while I didn't exactly use the pressure pump on Anton, I may have asked a few leadin' questions. Who was Stukey, where did he come from, and what was his idea—hirin' halls and so on? While Anton could recognize a dollar a long way off, he wasn't such a keen observer of folks.

"I don't worry whether he's a Wilson man or not," says Anton, "or which movie star he likes best after Mary Pickford. If I did I should ask Anna."

"Eh?" says I, sort of eager.

"He tells her a lot he don't tell me," says Anton.

"That's reasonable, too," says I. "Ask Anna. Say, that ain't a bad hunch. Much obliged."

It wasn't so easy, though, with Stukey on the job, to get near enough to ask Anna anything. When they came in, and

Anton invites me to join the fam'ly group in the boardin'-house dinin'-room while the cheese sandwiches and pickles was bein' passed around, I finds Stukey blockin' me off scientific.

As Anton had said, he had it bad. Never took his eyes off Anna for a second. I suppose he thought he was registerin' tender emotions, but it struck me as more of a hungry look than anything else. Miss Sobowski seemed to like it, though.

I expect a real lady's man wouldn't have had much trouble cuttin' in on Stukey and towin' Anna off into a corner. But that ain't my strong suit. The best I could do was to wait until the next day, when there was no opposition. Meantime I'd been usin' the long-distance reckless; so by the time Anna shows up at the Alcazar to open the window for the evenin' sale, I was primed with a good many more facts about a certain party than I had been the night before. Stukey wasn't quite such a man of mystery as he had been.

Course, I might have gone straight to Anton; but, somehow, I wanted to try out a few hints on Anna. I couldn't say just why, either. The line of josh I opens with ain't a bit subtle. It don't have to be. Anna was tickled to pieces to be kidded about her feller. She invites me into the box-office, offers me chewin' gum, and proceeds to get quite frisky.

"Ah, who was tellin' you that?" says she. "Can't a girl have a gentleman frien' without everybody's askin' is she engaged? Wotcher think?"

"Tut-tut!" says I. "I suppose, when you two had your heads together so close, he was rehearsin' one of his speeches to you—the kind he makes up in the hall, eh?"

"Mr. Stukey don't make no speeches there," says Anna. "He

just tells the others what to say. You ought to hear him talk, though. My, sometimes he's just grand!"

"Urgin' 'em not to quit work, I suppose?" says I.

"Him?" says Anna. "Not much. He wants 'em to strike, all the time strike, until they own the shops. He's got no use for rich people. Calls 'em blood-suckers and things like that. Oh, he's sump'n fierce when he talks about the rich."

"Is he?" says I. "I wonder why?"

"All the workers get like that," says Anna. "Mr. Stukey says that pretty soon everybody will join—all but the rich blood-suckers, and they'll be in jail. He was poor himself once. So was I, you know, in Poland. But we got along until the Germans came, and then—Ugh! I don't like to remember."

"Anton was tellin' me," says I. "You lost some of your folks."

"Lost!" says Anna, a panicky look comin' into her big eyes. "You call it that? I saw my father shot, my two brothers dragged off to work in the trenches, and my sister—oh, I can't! I can't say it!"

"Then don't tell Stukey," says I, "if you want to keep stringin' him along."

"But why?" demands Anna.

"Because," says I, "the money he's spendin' so free around here comes from them—the Germans."

"No, no!" says Anna, whisperin' husky. "That—that's a lie!"

"Sorry," says I; "but I got his number straight. He was workin' for a German insurance company up to 1915, bookkeepin' at ninety a month. Then he got the chuck. He came near starvin'. It was when he was almost in that he went crawlin' back to 'em, and they gave him this job. If you don't believe it's German money he's spendin' ask Anton to show you some of Stukey's canceled checks."

"But—but he's English," protests Anna. "Anyway, his father was."

"The Huns don't mind who they buy up," says I.

She's still starin' at me, sort of stunned.

"German money!" she repeats. "Him!"

"Anton will show you the checks," says I. "He don't care where they come from, so long as he can cash 'em. But you might hint to him that if another big strike is pulled it's apt to be a long one, and in that case the movie business will get a crimp put in it. The Warsaw receipts, too. I take it that Stukey's tryin' to work the hands up to a point where they'll vote for—"

"To-night they vote," breaks in Anna. "In two hours."

I lets out a whistle. "Zowie!" says I. "Guess I'm a little late. Say, you got a 'phone here. Would it do any good if you called Anton up and—"

"No," snaps Anna. "He thinks too slow. I must do this myself."

"You?" says I. "What could you do?"

"I don't know," says Anna. "But I must try. And quick. Hey, Marson! You—at the door. Come here and sell the tickets. Put an usher in your place."

With that she bounces down off the tall chair, shoves the substitute into her place, and goes streamin' out bare-headed. I decides to follow. But she leaves me behind as though I'd been standin' still.

At the Warsaw I finds Anton smokin' placid in his little office.

"Seen Anna?" I asks.

"Anna!" says he. "She should be selling tickets at the—"

"She was," says I; "but just now she's upstairs in the hall."

"At the meetin'?" gasps Anton. "Anna? Oh, no!"

"Come, take a look," says I.

And, for once in his life, Anton got a quick move on. He don't ask me to follow, but I trails along; and just as we strikes the top stair we hears a rousin' cheer go up. I suppose any other time we'd been barred out, but there's nobody to hold us up as we pushes through, for everyone has their eyes glued on the little stage at the far end of the hall.

No wonder. For there, standin' up before more than three hundred yellin' men, is this high-colored young woman.

Course, I couldn't get a word of it, my Polish education havin' been sadly neglected when I was young. But Anna seems to be tellin' some sort of story. My guess was that it's the one she'd hinted at to me—about her father and brothers and sister. But this time she seems to be throwin' in all the details.

There was nothin' frivolous about Anna's eyes now. It almost gave me a creepy feelin' to watch 'em—as if she was seein' things again that she'd like to forget—awful things. And she was makin' those three hundred men see the same things.

All of a sudden she breaks off, covers her face with her hands, and shivers. Then, quick as a flash, she turns and points to Stukey. I caught his name as she hisses it out. Stukey, turnin' a sickly yellow, slumps in his chair. Another second, and she's turned back to the men out front. She is puttin' something up to them—a question, straight from the shoulder.

The first to make a move is a squatty, thick-necked gent with one eye walled out. He jumps on a chair, shouts a few excited words, waves his long arms, and starts for the stage businesslike. The next thing I knew the riot was on, with Mortimer J. Stukey playin' the heavy lead and bein' tossed around like a rat.

It must have been Anton that switched off the lights and sent for the police. I didn't stop to ask. Bein' near the door, I felt my way downstairs and made a quick exit. Course, the ceremonies promised to continue interestin', but somehow this struck me as a swell time for me to quit. So I strolls back to the hotel and goes to bed.

Yes, I was some curious to know how the muss ended, but I didn't hurry around next mornin'. As a matter of fact, I'd enjoyed the society of the Sobowskis quite a lot durin' the past two days, and I thought I'd better stay away for a while. They're a strenuous bunch when they're stirred up—even a kittenish young thing like Anna.

About noon I 'phoned the works, and found that all was serene there, with no signs of a strike yet.

"No, and I got a hunch there won't be any, either," says I.

I was plannin' to linger in Bridgeport another day or so; but when the afternoon paper came out I changed my mind. Accordin' to the police-court reporter's account, there'd been some little disturbance in Warsaw Hall the night before. Seems a stranger by the name of Stukey had butted into a meetin' of the Pulaski Social Club, and had proceeded to get so messy that it had been found necessary to throw him out. Half a dozen witnesses told how rude he'd been, includin' the well-known citizen, Mr. Anton Sobowski, who owned the premises. The said Stukey had been a bit damaged; but after he'd been patched up at the City Hospital he'd been promised a nice long rest—thirty days, to be exact.

So I jumps the next train back to Broadway.

"Ah, Lieutenant!" says Mr. Ellins, glancin' up from his desk. "Find anything up there?"

"Uh-huh," says I. "His name was Stukey. Another case of drawin' his pay from Berlin."

"Hah!" grunts Old Hickory, bitin' into his cigar. "The long arm again. But can't you recommend something?"

"Sure!" says I. "If we could find a pair of gold boots about eighteen buttons high, we ought to send 'em to Anna Sobowski."

CHAPTER XI

AT THE TURN WITH WILFRED

I expect Mr. Robert overstated the case a bit. He was more or less hectic back of the ears about then, havin' just broken away after a half-hour session with Mrs. Stanton Bliss.

"That woman," says he, slumpin' into a chair and moppin' his brow, "has the mental equipment of a pet rabbit and the disposition of a setting hen. Good Lord!"

I looks over at Vee and grins. Had to. It ain't often you see Mr. Robert like that. And him bein' all dolled up in his nifty navy uniform made it seem just that much funnier. But Vee don't grin back. She'd sympathize with 'most anybody. At that exact minute, I'll bet she was bein' sorry for both of 'em all in the same breath, as you might say.

"But can't something be done—somehow?" she asks.

"Not by me," says Mr. Robert, decided. "Great marlinspikes! I'm not the war department, am I? I'm only a first-grade lieutenant in command of a blessed, smelly old menhaden trawler that's posing as a mine-sweeper. I am supposed to be enjoying a twenty-four hour shore leave in the peace and quiet of my home, and I get—this."

He waves his hand toward the other room, where the afore-mentioned Mrs. Stanton Bliss is sobbin, sniffin', and otherwise registerin' deep emotion by clawin' Mrs. Robert about the shoulders and wavin' away the smellin' salts.

"If it was the first time," growls Mr. Robert. "But it isn't."

That was true, too. You see, we'd heard somethin' about the other spasms. They'd begun along in July, when the awful news came out that Wilfred's red ink number had been plucked from the jar. Now you get it, don't you? Nothing unique. The same little old tragedy that was bein' staged in a million homes, includin' four-room flats, double-decker tenements, and boardin'-houses.

Only this happened to hit the forty-room country house of the Stanton Blisses. Course, it was different. Look who was bein' stirred up by it.

So mother had begun throwin' cat-fits. She'd tackled everyone she knew, demandin' to know what was to be done to keep Wilfred out of it. Among others, of course, she'd held up Mr. Robert. Wasn't he their nearest neighbor, and hadn't the Blisses entertained the Ellinses a lot? Not that she put it that way, exactly. But when she came with this hunch about gettin' sonny a snap job on some sort of naval construction work, why, of course, Mr. Robert couldn't duck. Yes, he thought he could place Wilfred. And he did—time-keeper, six-hour shift, and near enough so he could run back and forth every day in his machine.

That might have been good enough for some folks. It meant dodgin' the draft for Wilfred, dead sure. But mother didn't stay satisfied long. She went investigatin' around the plant. She found the office stuffy, Wilfred's desk had no electric fan on it, she wasn't sure of the drinkin' water, and the foreman was quite an impossible sort of person who always sneered when he had anything to say to Wilfred. Couldn't Mr. Robert attend to some of these things? Mr. Robert said he'd try—if he had time. He didn't get the time. More visits from mother.

Then this latest catastrophe. The Stanton Blisses had been away from home for three weeks or more, house-partyin' and motorin' through the mountains. Poor Wilfred had had to stay behind. What a stupidly distressin' thing war was, wasn't it? But he had been asked to spend his nights and Sundays with a college chum whose home was several miles nearer the works.

And then they had come back to find this scribbled note. Things had been gettin' worse and worse, Wilfred wrote. Some young hoodlums around the plant had shouted after him as he drove off in his car. Even young girls. The men had been surly to him, and that beastly foreman—Well, he wasn't goin' to stand for it, that was all. He didn't know just what he was goin' to do, but he was clearin' out. They'd hear from him later.

They had. This six-word message from Philadelphia, dated nearly two weeks ago, was also waitin'. It said that he'd enlisted, was all right, and for them not to worry. Nothin' more.

You couldn't blame mother for bein' stirred up. Her Wilfred had gone. Somewhere in some army camp or other, or at some naval trainin' station, the son and heir of the house of Bliss was minglin' with the coarse sons of the common people, was eatin' common food, was wearin' common clothes, was goin' up against the common thing generally. And that wasn't the worst of it. Where? Why didn't Mr. Robert tell her where? And couldn't he get him away at once? Mr. Robert had almost gone hoarse tryin' to explain why he couldn't. But after every try she'd come back with this wail:

"Oh, but you don't understand what it is to be a mother!"

"Thank the stars I don't!" says he, as he marches out of the room.

I was for clearin' out so he'd be free to shoo her in any style he wanted to. We'd been havin' dinner with the Ellinses, Vee and I, and it was time to go home anyway. But there's no budgin' Vee.

"Don't you think Torchy might find out where he is?" she suggests. "Bein' in the army himself, you know, and so clever at that sort of thing, I should think—"

"Why, to be sure," breaks in Mr. Robert, perkin' up all of a sudden and starin' at me. "Lieutenant Torchy to the rescue, of course. He's the very one."

"Ah, say, how'd you get that way?" says I. "Back up!"

He's off, though, callin' Mrs. Stanton Bliss. And before I can escape he's sickin' her on real enthusiastic. Also there's Vee urgin' me to see if I can't do something to locate Wilfred. So I had to make the stab.

"Got that wire with you?" I asks.

Yes, Mrs. Bliss had all the documents right handy. I takes the yellow sheet over under the readin' lamp and squints at it sleuthy, partly to kill time, and partly because I couldn't think of anything else to do. And of course they all have to gather round and watch me close, as if I was about to pull some miracle. Foolish! It was a great deal worse than that.

"H-m-m-m-m!" says I. "Philadelphia. I suppose there's some sort of naval trainin' station there, eh?"

Mr. Robert says there is.

"But if Wilfred was at it," I goes on, "and didn't want you to find him, he wouldn't have sent this from there, would he?"

Mrs. Stanton Bliss sighs. "I'm sure I don't know," says she. "I—I suppose not."

"Must be somewhere within strikin' distance of Philadelphia, though," says I. "Now, what camp is near?"

"Couldn't we wire someone in Washington and find out?" asks Mrs. Bliss.

"Sure," says I. "And we'd get an official answer from the Secretary of War about 11 A.M. next spring. It'll be a lot quicker to call up Whitey Weeks."

They don't know everything in newspaper offices, but there are mighty few things they can't find out. Whitey, though, didn't even have to consult the copy desk or the clippin' bureau.

"About the nearest big one," says he, "is the Ambulance Corps Camp at Allentown. Somewhere up on the Lehigh. S'long."

Here was another jolt for Mrs. Stanton Bliss. The Ambulance Corps! She near keeled over again, just hearin' me say it. Oh, oh! Did I really believe Wilfred could have been as rash as that?

"Why," says she, "they drive right up to the trenches, don't they? Isn't that fearfully dangerous?"

"War isn't a parlor pastime," puts in Mr. Robert. "And the ambulance drivers take their chances with the rest of the men. But there's no fightin' going on at Allentown. If Wilfred is there—"

"If he is," cuts in Mrs. Bliss, "I must go to him this very moment."

Some way that statement seemed to cheer Mr. Robert up a lot.

"Naturally," says he. "I'll look up a train for you. Just a second. In the A's. Allentown—Allen. Ah, page 156. M-m-m. Here you are. First one starts at 2 A.M. and gets you in at 5.15. Will that do?"

Mrs. Bliss turns on him sort of dazed, and blinks them round eyes of hers. She's a fairly well put up old girl, you know, built sort of on the pouter-pigeon type, but with good lines below the waist, and a complexion that she's taken lots of pains with. Dresses real classy, and, back to, she's often mistaken for daughter Marion. Travels in quite a gay bunch, I understand, with Mr. Stanton Bliss kind of trailin' along behind. Usually, when she ain't indulgin' in hysterics, she has very fetchin' kittenish ways. You know the kind. Their specialty's makin' the surroundin' males jump through the hoop for 'em. But when it comes to arrivin' anywhere at 5.15 A.M.—well, not for her.

"I should be a sight," says she.

"You'd still be a mother, wouldn't you?" asks Mr. Robert.

It was rough of him, as he was given to understand by the looks of all three ladies present, includin' Mrs. Robert; so he tries to square himself by lookin' up a ten o'clock train, all Pullman, with diner and observation.

"I would gladly take you up myself," says he, lyin' fluent, "if I didn't have to go back to my boat. But here is Torchy. He'll go, I suppose."

"Of course," says Vee.

And that's how I came to be occupyin' drawin'-room A, along with mother and sister Marion, as we breezes up into the Pennsylvania hills on this Wilfred hunt. A gushy, giggly young party Marion is, but she turns out to be quite a help. It was her who spots the two young soldiers driftin' through towards the smokin' compartment, and suggests that maybe they're goin' to the same camp.

"And they would know if Wilfred was there, wouldn't they?" she adds.

"Maybe," says I. "I'll go ask."

Nice, clean-cut young chaps they was. They'd stretched out comfortable on the leather seats, and was enjoyin' a perfectly good smoke, until I shows up. The minute I appears, though, they chucks their cigars and jumps up, heels together, right hand to the hat-brim. That's what I get by havin' this dinky bar on my shoulders.

"Can it, boys," says I. "This is unofficial."

"At ease, sir?" suggests one.

"As easy as you know how," says I.

Yes, they says they're ambulancers; on their way back to Allentown, too. But they didn't happen to know of any Wilfred Stanton Bliss there.

"You see, sir," says one, "there are about five thousand of us, so he might—"

"Sure!" says I. "But mother'll want an affidavit. Would you mind droppin' in and bein' cross-examined? There's sister Marion, too."

Obligin' chaps, they were; let me tow 'em into the drawin'-room, listened patient while Mrs. Bliss described just how Wilfred looked, and tried their best to remember havin' seen such a party. Also they gave her their expert opinion on how long the war was goin' to last, when Wilfred would be sent over, and what chances he stood of comin' back without a scratch.

Once more it was Marion who threw the switch.

"Tell me," says she, "will he be wearing a uniform just like yours?"

They said he would.

"Oh!" gurgles Marion, "I think it is perfectly spiffy. Don't you, mother? I'm just crazy to see Wilfred in one."

Mother catches the enthusiasm. "My noble boy!" says she, rollin' her eyes up.

From then on she's quite chipper. The idea of findin' sonny made over into a smart, dashin' soldier seemed to crowd out all the panicky thoughts she'd been havin'. From little hints she let drop, I judged that she was already picturin' him as a gallant hero, struttin' around haughty and givin' off stern commands. Maybe he'd been made a captain or something. Surely they would soon see that her Wilfred ought to be an officer of some kind.

"And we must have his portrait painted," she remarks, claspin' her hands excited as the happy thought strikes her.

The boys looked steady out of the window and managed to smother the smiles. I imagine they'd seen all sorts of mothers come to camp.

It's a lively little burg, Allentown, even if I didn't know it was on the map before. At the station you take a trolley that runs straight through the town and out to the fair grounds, where the camp is located. Goin' up the hill, you pass through the square and by the Soldiers' Monument. Say, it's some monument, too. Then out a long street lined with nice, comfortable-lookin' homes, until you get a glimpse of blue hills rollin' away as far as you can see, and there you are.

The boys piloted us past the guard at the gates, through a grove of trees, and left us at the information bureau, where a soldier wearin' shell-rimmed glasses listened patient while mother and sister both talked at once.

"Bliss? Just a moment," says he, reachin' for a card-index box. "Yes, ma'am. Wilfred Stanton. He's here."

"But where?" demands Mrs. Bliss.

"Why," says the soldier, "he's listed with the casuals just now. Quartered in the cow-barn."

"The—the cow-barn!" gasps Mrs. Bliss.

The soldier grins.

"It's over that way," says he, wavin' his hand. "Anyone will tell you."

They did. We wandered on and on, past the parade ground that used to be the trottin' track, past new barracks that was being knocked together hasty, until we comes to this dingy white buildin' with all the underwear hung up to dry around it. I took one glance inside, where the cots was stacked in thick and soldiers was loafin' around in various stages of dress and undress, and then I shooed mother and sister off a ways while I went scoutin' in alone. At a desk made out of a packin'-box I found a chap hammerin' away at a typewriter. He salutes and goes to attention.

"Yes, sir," says he, when I've told him who I'm lookin' for. "Squeaky Bliss. But he's on duty just now, sir."

I suggests that his mother and sister are here and would like to have a glimpse of him right away.

"They'd better wait until after five, sir," says he.

"I wouldn't like to try holdin' 'em in that long," says I.

"Very well, sir," says he. "Squeaky's on fatigue. Somewhere down at the further end of the grand stand you might catch him. But if it's his mother—well, I'd wait."

I passes this advice on to Mrs. Bliss.

"The idea!" says she. "I wish to see my noble soldier boy at once. Come."

So we went. There was no scarcity of young fellows in olive

drab. The place was thick with 'em. Squads were drillin' every way you looked, and out in the center of the field, where two or three hundred new ambulances were lined up, more squads were studyin' the insides of the motor, or practicin' loadin' in stretchers. Hundreds and hundreds of young fellows in uniform, all lookin' just alike. I didn't wonder that mother couldn't pick out sonny boy.

"What was it that man said?" she asks. "Wilfred on fatigue. Does that mean he is resting?"

"Not exactly," says I.

About then sister Marion begins to exhibit jumpy emotions.

"Mother! Mother!" says she, starin' straight ahead. "Look!"

All I could see was a greasy old truck backed up in front of some low windows under the grand stand, with half a dozen young toughs in smeary blue overalls jugglin' a load of galvanized iron cans. Looked like garbage cans; smelled that way too. And the gang that was handlin' 'em—well, most of 'em had had their heads shaved, and in that rig they certainly did look like a bunch from Sing Sing.

I was just nudgin' sister to move along, when Mrs. Bliss lets out this choky cry:

"Wilfred!" says she.

She hadn't made any mistake, either. It was sonny, all right. And you should have seen his face as he swings around and finds who's watchin' him. If it hadn't been for the bunkie who was helpin' him lift that can of sloppy stuff on to the tail of the truck, there'd been a fine spill, too.

"My boy! Wilfred!" calls Mrs. Stanton Bliss, holdin' out her arms invitin' and dramatic.

Now, in the first place, Wilfred was in no shape to be the party of the second part in a motherly clinch act. It's messy work, loadin' garbage cans, and he's peeled down for it. He was costumed in a pair of overalls that would have stood in the corner all by themselves, and an army undershirt with one sleeve half ripped off.

In the second place, all the rest of the bunch was wearin' broad grins, and he knew it. So he don't rush over at once. Instead he steps around to the front of the truck and salutes a husky, freckled-necked young sergeant who's sittin' behind the steerin' wheel.

"Family, sir," says Wilfred. "What—what'll I do?"

The sergeant takes one look over his shoulder.

"Oh, well," says he, "drop out until next load."

Not until Wilfred had led us around the corner does he express his feelin's.

"For the love of Mike, mother!" says he. "Wasn't it bad enough without your springin' that 'muh boy!' stuff? Right before all the fellows, too. Good-night!"

"But, Wilfred," insists mother, "what does this mean? Why do I find you—well, like this? Oh, it's too dreadful for words. Who has done this to you—and why?"

Jerky, little by little, Wilfred sketches out the answer. Army life wasn't what he'd expected. Not at all. He was sore on the whole business. He'd been let in for it, that was all. It wasn't so bad for some of the fellows, but they'd been lucky. As for him—well, he'd come here to learn to be an ambulance driver, and he had spent his first week in the kitchen, peelin' potatoes. Then, when they'd let him off that, and given him his first pass to go to town, just because he'd been a little late comin' back they'd jumped on him somethin' fierce. They'd shoved him on this garbage detail. He'd been on it ever since.

"It's that mucker of a top sergeant, Quigley," says Wilfred. "He's got it in for me."

Mrs. Stanton Bliss straightens out her chin dimple as she glares after the garbage truck, which is rollin' away in the distance.

"Has he, indeed!" says she. "We will see about that, then."

"But you must handle him easy, mother," warns Wilfred.

"That person!" snorts mother. "I shall have nothing to do with him whatever. I mean to get you out of this, Wilfred. I am going straight to the general."

"Now, mother!" protests Wilfred. "Don't make a scene."

When she was properly stirred up, though, that was mother's long suit. And she starts right in. Course, I tried to head her off, but it's no use. As there wasn't a general handy, she had to be satisfied with a major. Seemed like a mighty busy major, too; but when he heard his orderly tryin' to shunt the ladies, he gives the signal to let 'em in. You can bet I didn't follow. Didn't have to, for Mrs. Bliss wasn't doin' any whisperin' about then.

And she sure made it plain to the major how little she thought of the U. S. Army, and specially that part of it located at Allentown, Pa. Havin' got that off her chest, and been listened to patient, she demands that Wilfred be excused from all his disgustin' duties, and be allowed to go home with her at once and for good.

The major shakes his head. "Impossible!" says he.

"Then," says Mrs. Stanton Bliss, tossin' her head, "I shall appeal to the Secretary of War; to the President, if necessary."

The major smiles weary. "You'd best talk to his sergeant," says he. "If he recommends your son's discharge it may go through."

"That person!" exclaims Mrs. Bliss. "Never! I—I might talk to his captain."

"Useless, madam," says the major. "See his sergeant; he's the one."

And he signifies polite that the interview is over.

When mother tells sonny the result of this visit to headquarters, he shrugs his shoulders.

"I knew it would be that way," says he. "They've got me, and I've got to stand for it. No use askin' Quigley. You might as well go home."

"But at least you can get away long enough to have dinner with us," says mother.

"Nothing doin'," says Wilfred. "Can't get out unless Quigley signs a pass, and he won't."

"Oh, come!" says I. "He don't look so bad as all that. Let me see what I can do with him."

Well, after I'd chased the ladies back to the hotel with instructions to wait hopeful, I hunts up Top Sergeant Quigley. Had quite a revealin' chat with him, too. Come to look at him close after he'd washed up, he's rather decent appearin'. Face seems sort of familiar, too.

"Didn't you play first base for the Fordhams?" I asks.

"Oh, that was back in '14," says he.

"As I remember," says I, "you was some star on the bag, though. Now, about young Bliss. Case of mommer's pet, you know."

"He had that tag all over him," says Quigley. "But we're knockin' a lot of that out of him. He's comin' on."

"Good!" says I. "Would it stop the process to let him off for an evenin' with the folks—dinner and so on?"

"Why, no; I guess not," says Quigley. "Might do him good. But he must apply himself. Send him along."

So a half hour later I sat on a cot in the cow-barn and watched Wilfred, fresh from the shower bath, get into his army uniform.

"Say," he remarks, strugglin' through his khaki shirt, "I didn't think old Quig would do it."

"Seemed glad to," says I. "Said you was comin' on fine."

"He did?" gasps Wilfred. "Quigley? Well, what do you know!"

Not such a bad imitation of a soldier, Wilfred, when he'd laced up the leggins and got the snappy-cut coat buttoned tight. He's some different from what he was when sister first discovered him. And we had quite a gay dinner together.

First off mother was for campin' right down there indefinitely, where she could see her darlin' boy every day; but between Wilfred and me we persuaded her different. I expect the hotel quarters had something to do with it, too. Anyway, after Wilfred had promised to try for a couple of days off soon, for a visit home, she consents to start back in the mornin'.

"What I dread most, Wilfred," says she, "is leaving you at the mercy of that horrid sergeant."

"Oh, I'll get along with him somehow," says Wilfred. "I'm goin' to try, anyway."

And right there, as I understand it, Wilfred Stanton Bliss started to be a man and a soldier. He had a long way to go, though, it seemed to me.

So here the other day, only a couple of weeks since we made our trip, I'm some surprised to see who it is givin' me the zippy salute on the station platform out home. Yes, it's Wilfred. And say, he's got his shoulders squared, he's carryin' his chin up, and he's wearin' his uniform like it grew on him.

"Well, well!" says I. "Got your furlough, eh?"

"Yes, sir," says he. "Seventy-two hours. Had a whale of a time, too. You can't guess who I brought home with me, I'll bet."

I couldn't.

"Our top sergeant—Quigley," says he. "Say, he's all right. He's had us transferred to the best barracks in camp. Guess we deserve it, too, for we're on the way to bein' the crackerjack section of them all. You ought to see us drill. Some class! And it's all due to Quigley. Do you know what he thinks? That we're slated among the next lot to go over. How about that, sir? Won't that be great?"

"Huh!" says I. "How long ago was it you signed up, Wilfred?"

"Just six weeks, sir," says he.

"Whiffo!" says I, gawpin' at him. "If we had about a hundred thousand Quigleys!"

CHAPTER XII

VEE GOES OVER THE TOP

"But listen, Vee," says I. "If Hoover can't pull it off, with all the backin' he's got, what's the use of a few of you women mixin' in?"

"At least we can try," says Vee. "The prices this Belcher person is charging are something outrageous. Eggs ninety cents!"

"We should worry," says I. "Ain't we got nearly a hundred hens on the job?"

"But others haven't," says Vee. "Those people in that row of little cottages down by the station. The Walters, for instance. He can't get more than twenty-five or thirty dollars a week, can he?"

"There's so many cases you can't figure out," says I. "Maybe he scrubs along on small steaks or fried chicken."

"It's no joking matter," protests Vee. "Of course there are plenty of people worse off then the Walters. That Mrs. Burke, whose two boys are in the Sixty-ninth. She must do her marketing at Belcher's, too. Think of her having to pay those awful prices!"

"I would," says I, "if workin'up a case of glooms was any use; but I can't see—"

"We can see enough," breaks in Vee. "The new Belcher limousine, the additions to their hideous big house. All made, too, out of food profiteering right here. It's got to stop, that's all."

Which is where I should have shouted "Kamerad" and come runnin' out with my hands up, but I tried to show her that Belcher was only playin' the game like everyone else was playin' it.

"He ain't springin' anything new," says I. "He's just followin' the mob. They're all doin' it, from the Steel Trust down to the push-cart men. And when you come to interferin' with business—well, that's serious."

"Humph!" says Vee. "When it comes to taking advantage of poor people and depriving them of enough to eat, I call it plain piracy. And you ought to be ashamed of yourself, Torchy, standing up for such things."

So you see I was about as convincin' as a jazz band tryin' to imitate the Metropolitan orchestra doin' the overture to "Lucia." If I hadn't finally had sense enough to switch the subject a little, there might have been a poutin' scene and maybe a double case of sulks. But when I got to askin' where she'd collected all this grouch against our local meat and provision octopus, she cheers up again.

Seems she'd been to a Red Cross meetin' that afternoon, where a lot of the ladies was swappin' tales of woe about their kitchen expense accounts. Some of 'em had been keepin' track of prices in the city markets and was able to shoot the deadly parallel at Belcher. Anyway, they ditched the sweater-knittin' and bandage-rollin' for the time bein', and proceeded to organize the Woman's Economic League on the spot.

"Sounds impressive," says I. "And what then? Did you try Belcher for treason, find him guilty, and sentence him to be shot at sunrise?"

Vee proves that she's good-natured again by runnin' her tongue out at me.

"We did not, Smarty," says she. "But we passed a resolution condemning such extortion severely."

"How rough of you!" says I. "Anything else?"

"Yes," says Vee. "We appointed a committee to tell him he'd better stop."

"Fine!" says I. "I expect he'll have everything marked down about forty per cent. by to-morrow night."

Somehow, it didn't work out just that way. Next report I got from Vee was that the committee had interviewed Belcher, but there was nothing doin'. He'd been awfully nice to 'em, even if he had talked through his cigar part of the time.

Belcher says he feels just as bad as they about havin' to soak on such stiff prices. But how can he help it? The cold-storage people are boostin' their schedules every day. They ain't to blame, either. They're bein' held up by the farmers out West who are havin' their hair cut too often. Besides, all the hens in the country have quit layin' and joined the I. W. W., and every kind of meat is scarce on account of Pershing's men developin' such big appetites. He's sorry, but he's doin' his best, considerin' the war and everything. If people would only get the habit of usin' corn meal for their pie crusts, everything would be lovely once more.

"An alibi on every count," says I. "I expect the committee apologized."

"Very nearly that," says Vee. "The sillies! I just wish I'd been there. I don't believe half of what he said is true."

"That's one thing," says I, "but provin' it on him would be another. And there's where Belcher's got you."

Course, I like to watch Vee in action, for she sure is a humdinger when she gets started. As a rule, too, I don't believe in tryin' to block her off in any of her little enterprises.

But here was once where it seemed to me she was up against a hopeless proposition. So I goes on to point out, sort of gentle and soothin', how war prices couldn't be helped, any more'n you could stop the tide from comin' in.

Oh, I'm some smooth suggester, I am, when you get into fireside diplomacy. Anyway, the price of eggs wasn't mentioned again that evenin'. As a matter of fact, Vee ain't troubled much with marketin' details, for Madame Battou, wife of the little old Frenchman who does the cheffing for us so artistic, attends to layin' in the supplies. And, believe me, when she sails forth with her market basket you can be sure she's goin' to get sixteen ounces to the pound and the rock bottom price on everything. No 'phone orders for her. I don't believe Vee knew what the inside of Belcher's store looks like. I'm sure I didn't.

So I thought the big drive on the roast beef and canned goods sector had been called off. About that time, too, I got another inspection detail handed me,—and I didn't see my happy home until another week-end.

I lands back on Broadway at 9 A.M. Havin' reported at the Corrugated general offices and found Old Hickory out of town, I declares a special holiday and beats it out to the part of Long Island I'm beginnin' to know best. Struck me Professor Battou held his face kind of funny when he saw me blow in; and as I asks for Vee, him and the madam swaps glances. He say she's out.

"Oh," says I. "Mornin' call up at the Ellinses', eh? I'll stroll up that way, myself, then."

Leon hesitates a minute, like he was chokin' over something, and then remarks: "But no, M'sieur. Madame, I think, is in the village."

"Why," says I, "I just came from the station. I didn't see the car around. How long has she been gone?"

Another exchange of looks, and then Battou answers:

"She goes at seven."

"Whaddye mean goes?" says I. "It ain't a habit of hers, is it?"

Leon nods.

"All this week," says he. "She goes to the meat and grocery establishment, I understand."

"Belcher's?" says I. "But what—what's the idea?"

"I think it would be best if M'sieur asked Madame," says he.

"That's right, too," says I.

You can guess I was some puzzled. Was Vee doin' the spy act on Belcher, watchin' him open the store and spendin' the forenoon concealed in a crockery crate or something? No, that didn't sound reasonable. But what the—Meanwhile I was leggin' it down towards the village.

It's a busy place, Belcher's, specially on Saturday forenoon. Out front three or four delivery trucks was bein' loaded up, and inside a lot of clerks was jumpin' round. Among the customers was two Jap butlers, three or four Swedish maids, and some of the women from the village. But no Vee anywhere in sight.

Loomin' prominent in the midst of all this active tradin' is Belcher himself, a thick-necked, ruddy-cheeked party, with bristly black hair cut shoe-brush style and growing down to a point in front. His big, bulgy eyes are cold and fishy, but they seem to take in everything that's goin' on. I hadn't been standin' around more'n half a minute before he snaps his finger, and a clerk comes hustlin' over to ask what I'll have.

"Box of ginger-snaps," says I offhand; and a minute later I'm bein' shunted towards a wire-cage with a cash slip in my hand.

I'd dug up a quarter, and was waitin' for the change to be passed out through the little window, when I hears a familiar snicker. Then I glances in to see who's presidin' at the cash register. And say, of all the sudden jolts I ever got! It's Vee.

"Well, for the love of soup!" I gasps.

"Twelve out—thirteen. That's right, isn't it? Thank you so much, sir," says she, her gray eyes twinklin'.

"Quit the kiddin'," says I, "and sketch out the plot of the piece."

"Can't now," says Vee. "So run along. Please!"

"But how long does this act of yours last?" I insists.

"Until about noon, I think," says she. "It's such fun. You can't imagine."

"What's it for, though?" says I. "Are you pullin' a sleuth stunt on—"

"S-s-s-sh!" warns Vee. "He's coming. Pretend to be getting a bill changed or something."

It's while I'm fishin' out a ten that this little dialogue at the meat counter begins to get conspicuous: A thin, stoop-shouldered female with gray streaks in her hair is puttin' up a howl at the price of corned beef. She'd asked for the cheapest piece they had, and it had been weighed for her, but still she wasn't satisfied.

"It wasn't as high last Saturday," she objects.

"No, ma'am," says the clerk. "It's gone up since."

"Worse luck," says she, pokin' the piece with her finger. "And this is nearly all bone and fat. Now couldn't you—"

"I'll ask the boss, ma'am," says the clerk. "Here he is."

Belcher has come over and is listenin', glarin' hostile at the woman.

"It's Mrs. Burke, the one whose sons are in the army,"

whispers Vee.

"Well?" demands Belcher.

"It's so much to pay for meat like that," says Mrs. Burke. "If you could—"

"Take it or leave it," snaps Belcher.

"Sure now," says she, "you know I can't afford to give—"

"Then get out!" orders Belcher.

At which Vee swings open the door of the cage, brushes past me, and faces him with her eyes snappin'.

"Pig!" says she explosive.

"Wha-a-a-at!" gasps Belcher, gawpin' at her.

"I—I beg pardon," says Vee. "I shouldn't have said that, even if it was so."

"You—you're discharged, you!" roars Belcher.

"Isn't that nice?" says Vee, reachin' for her hat and coat. "Then I can go home with my husband, I suppose. And if I have earned any of that princely salary—five dollars a week, it was to be, wasn't it?—well, you may credit it to my account: Mrs. Richard Tabor Ballard, you know. Come, Torchy."

Say, I always did suspect there was mighty few things Vee was afraid of, but I never thought she had so much clear grit stowed away in her system. For to sail past Belcher the way he looked then took a heap of nerve, believe me. But before he can get that thick tongue of his limbered up we're outside, with Vee snuggled up mufflin' the giggles against my coat sleeve.

"Oh, it's been such a lark, Torchy!" says she. "I've passed as Miss Hemmingway for six days, and I don't believe more than three or four persons have suspected. Thank goodness, Belcher wasn't one of them. For I've learned—oh, such a lot!"

"Let's start at the beginning," says I. "Why did you do it at all?"

"Because the committee was so ready to believe the whoppers he told," says Vee. "And they wanted to disband the League, especially that Mrs. Norton Plummer, whose husband is a lawyer. She was almost disagreeable about it. Truly. 'But, my dear,' she said to me, 'one can't act merely on rumor and prejudice. If we had a few facts or figures it might be different.' And you know that sour smile of hers. Well! That's why I did it. I asked them to give me ten days. And now—"

Vee finishes by squeezin' my arm.

"But how'd you come to break in so prompt?" I asks. "Did you mesmerize Belcher?"

"I bought up his cashier—paid her to report that she was ill," says Vee. "Then I smoothed back my hair, put on this old black dress, and went begging for the job. That's when I began to know Mr. Belcher. He's quite a different person when he is hiring a cashier from the one you see talking to customers. Really, I've never been looked at that way before—as if I were some sort of insect. But when he found I would work cheap, and could get Mrs. Robert Ellins to go on

Sewell Ford

my bond if I should turn out a thief, he took me on.

"Getting up so early was a bit hard, and eating a cold luncheon harder still; but worst of all was having to hear him growl and snap at the clerks. Oh, he's perfectly horrid. I don't see how they stand it. Of course, I had my share. 'Miss Blockhead' was his pet name for me."

"Huh!" says I, grittin' my teeth.

"Meaning that you'd like to tell Belcher a few things yourself?" asks Vee. "Well, you needn't. I'd no right to be there, for one thing. And, for another, this is my own particular affair. I know what I am going to do to Mr. Belcher; at least, what I'm going to try to do. Anyway, I shall have some figures to put before our committee Monday. Then we shall see."

Yep, she had the goods on him. I helped her straighten out the evidence: copies of commission-house bills showin' what he had paid for stuff, and duplicates of sales-slips givin' the retail prices he got. And say, all he was stickin' on was from thirty to sixty per cent. profit.

He didn't always wait for the wholesaler to start the boostin', either. Vee points out where he has jacked up the price three times on the same shipment—just as the spell took him. He'd be readin' away in his *Morgen Blatherskite*, and all of a sudden he'd jump out of his chair. I'm no expert on provision prices, but some of them items had me bug-eyed.

"Why," says I, "it looks like this Belcher party meant to discourage eatin' altogether. Couldn't do better if he was runnin' a dinin'-car."

"It's robbery, that's what it is," says Vee. "And when you

think that his chief victims are such helpless people as the Burkes and the Walters—well, it's little less than criminal."

"It's a rough deal," I admits, "but one that's bein' pulled in the best circles. War profits are what everybody seems to be out after these days, and I don't see how you're going to stop it."

"I mean to try to stop Belcher, anyway," says Vee, tossin' her chin up.

"You ain't got much show," says I; "but go to it."

Just how much fight there was in Vee, though, I didn't have any idea of until I saw her Monday evenin' after another meetin' of the League. It seems she'd met this Mrs. Norton Plummer on her own ground and had smeared her all over the map.

"What do you suppose she wanted to do?" demands Vee. "Pass more resolutions! Well, I told her just what I thought of that. As well pin a 'Please-keep-out' notice on your door to scare away burglars as to send resolutions to Belcher. And when I showed her what profits he was making, item by item, she hadn't another word to say. Then I proposed my plan."

"Eh?" says I. "What's it like?"

"We are going to start a store of our own," says Vee—just like that, offhand and casual.

"You are!" says I. "But—but who's goin' to run it?"

"They made me chairman of the sub-committee," says Vee. "And then I made them subscribe to a campaign fund. Five thousand. We raised it in as many minutes. And now—well,

I suppose I'm in for it."

"Listens that way to me," says I.

"Then I may as well begin," says she.

And say, there's nothin' draggy about Vee when she really goes over the top. While I'm dressin' for dinner she calls up a real estate dealer and leases a vacant store in the other end of the block from Belcher's. Between the roast and salad she uses the 'phone some more and drafts half a dozen young ladies from the Country Club set to act as relay clerks. Later on in the evenin' she rounds up Major Percy Thomson, who's been invalided home from the Quartermaster's Department on account of a game knee, and gets him to serve as buyin' agent for a week or so. Her next move is to charter a couple of three-ton motor-trucks to haul supplies out from town; and when I went to sleep she was still jottin' things down on a pad to be attended to in the mornin'.

For two or three days nothin' much seemed to happen. The windows of that vacant store was whitened mysterious, carpenters were hammerin' away inside, and now and then a truck backed up and was unloaded. But no word was given out as to what was goin' to be sprung. Not until Friday mornin'. Then the commuters on the 8.03 was hit bang in the eye by a whalin' big red, white, and blue sign announcin' that the W. E. L. Supply Company was open for business.

Course, it was kind of crude compared to Belcher's. No fancy counters or showcases or window displays of cracker-boxes. And the stock was limited to staples that could be handled easy. But the price bulletins posted up outside was what made some of them gents who'd been doin' the fam'ly marketin' stop and stare. A few of 'em turned halfway to the station and dashed back to leave their orders. Goin' into town they spread the news through the train. The story of that latest bag of U-boats, which the mornin' papers all carried screamers about, was almost thrown into the discard. If I hadn't been due for a ten o'clock committee meetin' at the Corrugated, I'd have stayed out and watched the openin'. Havin' told Old Hickory about it, though, I was on hand next mornin' with a whole day's furlough.

"It ought to be our big day," says Vee.

It was. For one thing, everybody was stockin' up for over Sunday, and with the backin' of the League the Supply Company could count on about fifty good customers as a starter. Most of the ladies came themselves, rollin' up in limousines or tourin' cars and cartin' home their own stuff. Also the cottage people, who'd got wind of the big mark-down bargains, begun to come in bunches, every woman with a basket.

But they didn't swamp Vee. She'd already added to her force of young lady clerks a squad of hand-picked Boy Scouts, and it was my job to manage the youngsters.

I'd worked out the system the night before. Each one had typed price lists in his pocket, and besides that I'd put 'em through an hour's drill on weights and measures before the show started.

I don't know when it was Belcher begun to get wise and start his counter-attack; but the first time I had a chance to slip out and take a squint his way, I saw this whackin' big sign in front of his place: "Potatoes, 40 cents per peck." Which I promptly reports to Vee.

"Very well," says she; "we'll make ours thirty-five."

Inside of ten minutes we had a bulletin out twice as big as his.

"Now I guess he'll be good," says I.

But he had a scrap or two left in him, it seems. Pretty soon he cuts the price to thirty.

"We'll make it twenty-five," says Vee.

And by eleven o'clock Belcher has countered with potatoes at twenty cents.

"Why," gasps Vee, "that's far less than they cost at wholesale. But we can't let him beat us. Make ours twenty, too."

"Excuse me, ma'am," puts in one of the Scouts, salutin', "but we've run out of potatoes."

"Oh, boy!" says I. "Where do we go from here!"

Vee hesitates only long enough to draw a deep breath.

"Torchy," says she, "I have it. Form your boys into a basket brigade, and buy out Belcher below the market."

Talk about your frenzied finance! Wasn't that puttin' it over on him! For two hours, there, we went long on Belcher's potatoes at twenty, until his supply ran out too. Then he switched to sugar and butter. Quotations went off as fast as when the bottom drops out of a bull market. All we had to do to hammer down the prices of anything in the food line, whether we had it or not, was to stick out a cut-rate sign— Belcher was sure to go it one better; and when Vee got it far enough below cost, she started her buyin' corps, workin' in customers, clerks, and anybody that was handy. And by night if every fam'ly within five miles hadn't stocked up on bargain provisions it was their own fault; for if they didn't have cash of their own Vee was right there with the long-distance credit.

"I'll bet you've got old Belcher frothin' through his ears," says I.

"I hope so," says Vee.

The followin' Monday, though, he comes back at her with his big push. He had the whole front of his store plastered with below-cost bulletins.

"Pooh!" says Vee. "I can have signs like that painted, too."

And she did. It didn't bother her a bit if her stock ran out. She kept up on the cut-rate game, and when people asked for things she didn't have she just sent 'em to Belcher's.

Maybe you saw what some of the papers printed. Course, they joshed the ladies more or less, but also they played up a peppery interview with Belcher which got him in bad with everybody. Vee wasn't so pleased at the publicity stuff, but she didn't squeal.

What was worryin' me some was how soon the grand smash was comin'. I knew that the campaign fund had been whittled into considerable, and now that prices had been slashed there was no chance for profits.

It was botherin' Vee some, too, for she'd promised not to assess the League members again unless she could show 'em where they were comin' out. By the middle of the week things looked squally. Belcher had given out word that he meant to bust up this fool woman's opposition, if it took his last cent.

Then, here the other night, I comes home to find Vee wearin' a satisfied grin. As I comes in she jumps up from her desk and waves a check at me.

"Look!" says she. "Five thousand! I've got it back, Torchy, every dollar."

"Eh?" says I. "You ain't sold out to Belcher?"

"I should say not," says she. "To the Noonan chain. Mr. Noonan came himself. He'd read about our fight in the newspapers, and said he'd be glad to take it off our hands. He's been wanting to establish a branch in this district. Five thousand for stock and good will. What do you think of that?"

"I ain't thinkin'," says I. "I'm just gaspin' for breath. Noonan, eh? Then I see where Belcher gets off. And if you don't mind my whisperin' in your ear, Vee, you're some whizz."

CHAPTER XIII

LATE RETURNS ON RUPERT

Vee and I were goin' over some old snapshots the other night. It's done now and then, you know. Not deliberate. I'll admit that's a pastime you wouldn't get all worked up over plannin' ahead for. Tuesday mornin', say, you don't remark breathless: "I'll tell you: Saturday night at nine-thirty let's get out them last year's prints and give 'em the comp'ny front."

It don't happen that way—not with our sketch. What I was grapplin' for in the bottom of the window-seat locker was something different—maybe a marshmallow fork, or a corn-popper, or a catalogue of bath-room fixtures. Anyway, it was something we thought we wanted a lot, when I digs up this album of views that Vee took durin' that treasure-huntin' cruise of ours last winter on the old *Agnes*, with Auntie and Old Hickory and Captain Rupert Killam and the rest of the bunch. I was just tossin' the book one side when a picture slips out, and of course I has to take a squint. Then I chuckles.

"Look!" says I, luggin' it over to where Vee is curled up on the davenport in front of the fireplace. "Remember that?"

A giggle from Vee.

"'Auntie enjoying a half-hour eulogy of the dear departed, by Mrs. Mumford,' should be the title," says she. "She'd been sound asleep for twenty minutes."

"Which is what you might call good defensive," says I. "But who's this gazin' over the rail beyond—J. Dudley Simms, or is that a ventilator?"

"Let's see," says Vee, reachin' for the readin' glass. "Why, you silly! That's Captain Killam."

"Oh!" says I. "Reckless Rupert, the great mind-play hero."

"I wonder what has become of him?" puts in Vee, restin' her chin on the knuckle of her forefinger and starin' into the fire.

"Him?" says I. "Most likely he's back in St. Petersburg, Florida, all dolled in white flannels, givin' the tin-can tourists a treat. That would be Rupert's game."

I don't know as you remember; but, in spite of Killam's havin' got balled up on the location of this pirate island, and Vee and me havin' to find it for him, he came in for his share of the loot. Must have been quite a nice little pot for Rupert, too—enough to keep him costumed for his mysterious hero act for a long time, providin' he don't overdress the part.

Weird combination—Rupert: about 60 per cent. camouflage and the rest solemn boob. An ex-school-teacher from some little flag station in middle Illinois, who'd drifted down to the West Coast, and got to be a captain by ownin' an old cruiser that he took fishin' parties out to the grouper banks on. Them was the real facts in the life story of Rupert.

But the picture he threw on the screen of himself must have been something else again—seasoned sailor, hardy adventurer, daredevil explorer, and who knows what else? Catch him in one of his silent, starey moods, with them buttermilk blue eyes of his opened wide and vacant, and you had the outline. But that's as far as you'd get. I always thought Rupert himself was a little vague about it, but he would insist on takin' himself so serious. That's why we never got along well, I expect. To me Rupert was a walkin' joke, except when he got to sleuthin' around Vee and me and made a nuisance of himself.

"How completely people like that drop out of sight sometimes," says Vee, shuttin' up the album.

"Yes," says I. "Contrary to old ladies who meet at summer resorts and in department-stores, it's a sizable world we live in. Thanks be for that, too."

But you never can tell. It ain't more'n three days later, as I'm breezin through a cross street down in the cloak-and-suit and publishin' house district, when a taxi rolls up to the curb just ahead, and out piles a wide-shouldered gent with freckles on the back of his neck. Course, I don't let on I can spot anybody I've ever known just by a sectional glimpse like that. But this was no common case of freckles. This was a splotchy, spattery system of rust marks, like a bird's-eye view of the enemy's trenches after a week of drum fire. Besides, there was the pale carroty hair.

Even then, the braid-bound cutaway and the biscuit-colored spats had me buffaloed. So I slows up until I can get a front view of the party who's almost tripped himself with the horn-handled walkin'-stick and is havin' a few last words with someone in the cab. Then I sees the washed out blue eyes, and I know there can't be any mistake. About then, too, he turns and recognizes me.

"Well, for the love of beans!" says I. "Rupert!"

The funny part of it is that I gets it off as cordial as if I was discoverin' an old trench mate. You know how you will. And, while I can't say Captain Killam registered any wild joy in his greetin', still he seemed pleased enough. He gives me a real hearty shake.

"And here is someone else you know," says he, wavin' to the cab: "Mrs. Mumford."

Blamed if it ain't the cooin' widow. She's right there with the old familiar purry gush, too, squeezin' my fingers kittenish and askin' me how "dear, sweet Verona" is. I was just noticin' that she'd ditched the half mournin' for some real zippy raiment when she leans back so as to exhibit a third party in the taxi—a young gent with one of these dead-white faces and a cute little black mustache—reg'lar lounge-lizard type.

"Oh, and you must meet my dear friend, Mr. Vinton Bartley," she purrs. "Vinton, this is the Torchy I've spoken about so often."

"Ah, ya-a-as," drawls Vinton, blowin' out a whiff of scented cigarette smoke lazy. "Quite so. But—er—hadn't we best be getting on, Lorina?"

"Yes, yes," coos Mrs. Mumford. "By-by, Captain. Good-by, Torchy."

And off they whirls, leavin' me with my mouth open and Rupert starin' after 'em gloomy.

"Lorina, eh?" says I. "How touchin'!"

Killam only grunts, but it struck me he has tinted up a bit under the eyes.

"Say, Rupert," I goes on, "who's your languid friend with the cream-of-cabbage complexion?"

"Bartley?" says he. "Oh, he's a friend of Mrs. Mumford; a drama-tist—so he says."

Now, I might have let it ride at that and gone along about my own affairs, which ain't so pressin' just then. Yes, I might. But I don't. Maybe it was hornin' in where there was no welcome sign on the mat, and then again perhaps it was only a natural folksy feelin' for an old friend I hadn't seen for a long time. Anyway, I'm prompted sudden to take Rupert by the arm and insist that he must come and have lunch with me.

"Why—er—thanks," says the Captain; "but I have a little business to attend to in here." And he nods to an office buildin'.

"That'll be all right, too," says I. "I'll wait."

"Will you?" says Rupert, beamin'. "I shall be pleased."

So in less'n half an hour I have Rupert planted cozy at a corner table with a mixed grill in front of him, and I'm givin' him the cue for openin' any confidential chat he may have on hand. He's a good deal of a clam, though, Rupert. And suspicious! He must have been born lookin' over his shoulder. But in my own crude way I can sometimes josh 'em along.

"Excuse me for mentionin' it, Rupert," says I, "but there's lots of class to you these days."

"Eh?" says he. "You mean—"

"The whole effect," says I, "from the gaiters to the new-model lid. Just like you'd strolled out from some Fifth Avenue club and was goin' to 'phone your brokers to buy another block of Bethlehem at the market. Honest!"

He pinks up and shakes his head, but I can see I've got the range.

"And here Vee and I had it doped out," I goes on, "how you'd be down on the West Coast by this time, investin' your pile in orange groves and corner lots."

"No," says Rupert; "I've been here all the while. You see, I— I've grown rather fond of New York."

"You needn't apologize," says I. "There's a few million others with the same weakness, not countin' the ones that sleep in New Jersey but always register from here. Gone into some kind of business, have you?"

Rupert does some fancy side-steppin' about then; but all of a sudden he changes his mind, and, after glancin' around to see that no one has an ear out, he starts his confession.

"The fact is," says he, "I've been doing a little literary work."

"Writin' ads," says I, "or solicitin' magazine subscriptions?"

"I am getting out a book of poems," says Rupert, dignified.

"Wh-a-a-at?" I gasps. "Not—not reg'lar limerick stuff?"

I can see now that was a bad break. But Rupert was patient with me. He explains that these are all poems about sailors and ships and so on; real salt, tarry stuff. Also, he points out how it's built the new style way, with no foolish rhymes at the end, and with long lines or short, just as they happen to come. To make it clear, he digs up a roll of galley proofs he's just collected from the publishers. And say, he had the goods. There it was, yards of it, all printed neat in big fat type. "Sea Songs" is what he calls 'em, and each one has a separate tag of its own, such as "Kittywakes," "Close Hauled," and "Scuppers Under."

"Looks like the real stuff," says I. "Let's hear how it listens. Ah, come on! Some of that last one, about scuppers, now."

With a little more urgin', Rupert reads it to me. I should call him a good reader, too. Anyway, he can untie one of them deep, boomin' voices, and with that long, serious face of his helpin' out the general effect—well, it's kind of impressive. He spiels off two or three stickfuls and then stops.

"Which way was you readin' that, backwards or forwards?" says I.

Rupert begins to stiffen up, and I hurries on with the apology. "My mistake," says I. "I thought maybe you might have got mixed at the start. No offense. But say, Cap'n, what's the big idea? What does it all mean?"

In some ways Rupert is good-natured. He was then. He explains how in this brand of verse you don't try to tell a story or anything like that. "I am merely giving my impressions," says he. "That is all. Interpreting my own feelings, as it were."

"Oh!" says I. "Then there's no goin' behind the returns. Who's to say you don't feel that way? I get you now. But that ain't the kind of stuff you can wish onto the magazines, is it?"

Which shows just how far behind the bass-drum I am. Rupert tells me the different places where he's unloaded his pieces, most of 'em for real money. Also, I pumps out of him how he came to get into the game. Seems he'd been roomin' down in old Greenwich Village; just happened to drift in among them long-haired men and short-haired girls. It turns out that the book was a little enterprise that was being backed by Mrs. Mumford. Yes, it's that kind of a book—so much down in advance to the Grafter Press. You know, Mrs. Mumford always did fall for Rupert, and after she's read one of his sea spasms in a magazine she don't lose any time huntin' him out and renewin' their cruise acquaintance. A real poet! Say, I can just see her playin' that up among her friends. And when she finds he's mixin' in with all those dear, delightful Bohemians, she insists that Rupert tow her along too.

From then on it was a common thing for her and Rupert to go browsin' around among them garlic and red-ink joints, defyin' ptomaines and learnin' to braid spaghetti on a fork. That was her idea of life. She hires an apartment right off Washington Square and moves in from Montclair for the winter. She begun to have what she called her "salon evenings," when she collected any kind of near-celebrity she could get.

Mr. Vinton Bartley was generally one of the favored guests. I didn't need any second sight, either, to suspect that Vinton was sort of crowdin' in on this little romance of Rupert's. And by eggin' Rupert along judicious I got the whole tale.

Seems it had been one of Mrs. Mumford's ambitions to spring Rupert on an unsuspectin' public. Her idea is to have Rupert called on, some night at the Purple Pup, to step up to the head of the long table and give one of his sea songs. She'd picked Vinton to do the callin'. And Vinton had balked.

"But say," says I, "is this Vinton gent the only one of her friends that's got a voice? Why not pick another announcer?"

"I'm sure I don't know," says Rupert. "She—she hasn't mentioned the subject recently."

"Oh!" says I. "Too busy listenin' to the voice of the viper, eh?"

Rupert nods and stares sad into his empty demi-tasse. And, say, when Rupert gets that way he's an appealin' cuss.

"See here, Rupert," says I; "if you got a call of that kind, would you come to the front and make a noise like a real poet?"

"Why," says he, "I suppose I ought to. It would help the sale of the book, and perhaps—"

"One alibi is enough," I breaks in. "Now, another thing: How'd you like to have me stage-manage this debut of yours?"

"Oh, would you?" says he, beamin'.

"Providin' you'll follow directions," says I.

"Why, certainly," says Rupert. "Any suggestions that you may make—"

"Then we'll begin right now," says I. "You are to ditch that flossy floor-walker outfit of yours from this on."

"You mean," says Rupert, "that I am not to wear these clothes?"

"Just that," says I. "When you get to givin' mornin' readin's at the Plaza for the benefit of the Red Cross, you can dig 'em out again; but for the Purple Pup you got to be costumed different. Who ever heard of a goulash poet in a braid-bound cutaway and spats? Say, it's a wonder they let you live south of the Arch."

"But—but what ought I to wear?" asks Rupert.

"Foolish question!" says I. "Who are you, anyway? Answer: the Sailor Poet. There you are! Sea captain's togs for you—double-breasted blue coat, baggy-kneed blue trousers, and a yachtin' cap."

"Very well," says Rupert. "But about my being asked to read. Just how—"

"Leave it to me, Rupert," says I. "Leave everything to me."

Which was a lot simpler than tellin' him I didn't know.

You should have seen Vee's face when I tells her about Rupert's new line.

"Captain Killam a poet!" says she. "Oh, really now, Torchy!"

"Uh-huh!" says I. "He's done enough for a book. Read me some of it, too."

"But—but what is it like?" asks Vee. "How does it sound?"

"Why," says I, "it sounds batty to me—like a record made by a sailor who was simple in the head and talked a lot in his sleep. Course, I'm no judge. What's the difference, though? Rupert wants to spout it in public."

"But the people in the restaurant," protests Vee. "Suppose they should laugh, or do something worse?"

"That's where Rupert is takin' a chance," says I. "Personally, I think he'll be lucky if they don't throw plates at him. But we ain't underwritin' any accident policy; we're just bookin' him for a part he claims he can play. Are you on?"

Vee gets that eye twinkle of hers workin'. "I think it will be perfectly lovely."

I got to admit, too, that she's quite a help.

"We must be sure Mrs. Mumford and that Bartley person are both there," says she. "And we ought to have as many of Captain Killam's friends as possible. I'll tell you. Let's give a dinner-party."

"Must we?" says I. "You know we ain't introducin' any London success. This is Rupert's first stab, remember."

We set the date for the day the book was to be out, which gives Rupert an excuse for celebratin'. He'd invited Mrs. Mumford and Vinton to be his guests, and they'd promised to be on hand. As for us, we'd rounded up Mr. and Mrs. Robert Ellins and J. Dudley Simms.

Well, everybody showed up. And as it happens, it's one of the big nights at the Purple Pup. The long center table is surrounded by a gay bunch of assorted artists who are bein' financed by an out-of-town buyer who seems to be openin' Chianti reckless. We were over in one corner, as far away from the ukulele torturers as we could get, while at the other end of the room is Rupert with his two. I thought he looked kind of pallid, but it might have been only on account of the cigarette smoke.

"Is it time yet, Torchy?" asks Mr. Robert, when we gets through to the striped ice cream and chicory essence.

"Let's hold off," says I, "and see if someone else don't pull a curtain-raiser."

Sure enough, they did. A bald-headed, red-faced old boy with a Liberty Bond button in his coat-lapel insists on everybody's drinkin' to our boys at the front. Followin' that, someone leads a slim, big-eyed young female to the piano and announces that she will do a couple of Serbian folk-songs. Maybe she did. I hope the Serbs forgive her.

"If they can take that without squirmin'," says I, "I guess they can stand for Rupert. Go on, Mr. Robert. Shoot."

Course, he's no spellbinder, but he can say what he wants to in a few words and make himself heard. And then, bein' in naval uniform helped.

"I think we have with us to-night," says he, "Captain Rupert Killam, the sailor poet. I should like, if it pleases the company, to ask Captain Killam to read for us some of his popular verses. Does anyone second the motion?"

"Killam! Killam!" roars out the sporty wine-opener.

Others took up the chorus, and in the midst of it I dashes over to drag Rupert from his chair if necessary.

But I wasn't needed. As a matter of fact, he beat me to it. Before I could get half way to him, he is standin' at the end of the long table, his eyes dropped modest, and a brand-new volume of "Sea Songs" held conspicuous over his chest.

"This is indeed an unexpected honor," says Rupert, lyin'

fluent. "I am a plain sailor-man, as you know, but if you insist—"

And, before they could hedge, he has squared his shoulders, thrown his head well back, and has cut loose with that boomin' voice of his. Does he put it over? Say, honest, I finds myself listenin' with my mouth open, just as though I understood every word. And the first thing I know he's carryin' the house with him. Even some of the Hungarian waiters stopped to see what it's all about.

> Tides!
> Little, rushing, hurrying tides
> Along the sloping deck.
> And the bobstay smashing the big blue deep,
> While under my hand
> The kicking tiller groans
> Its oaken soul out in a gray despair.

That's part of it I copied down afterward. Yet that crowd just lapped it up.

"Wow!" "Brava! Brava!" "What's the matter with Killam?" they yells. "More!"

Rupert was flushin' clear up the back of his neck now. Also he was fumblin' with the book, hesitatin' what to give 'em next, when I pushes in and begins pumpin' his hand.

"Shall—shall I—" he starts to ask.

"No, you boob," I whispers. "Quit while the quittin's good. You got 'em buffaloed, all right. Let it ride."

And I fairly shoves him over to his table, where Sister Mumford has already split out a new pair of gloves and is beamin' joyous, while Vinton is sittin' there with his chin on his necktie, lookin' like someone had beaned him with a bung-starter.

But we wasn't wise just how strong Rupert had scored until we saw the half page Whitey Weeks had gotten out of it for the Sunday paper. "New Poet Captures Greenwich Village" is the top headline, and there's a three-column cut showin' Rupert spoutin' his "Sea Songs" through the cigarette smoke. Also, I gather from a casual remark Rupert let drop yesterday that the prospects of him and Mrs. Mumford enterin' the mixed doubles class soon are good. And, with her ownin' a big retail coal business over in Jersey, I expect Rupert can go on writin' his pomes as free as he likes.

CHAPTER XIV

FORSYTHE AT THE FINISH

I expect I wouldn't have noticed Forsythe particular if it hadn't been for Mrs. Robert. It takes all kinds, you know, to make up a week-end house-party bunch; and in these days, when specimens of the razor-usin' sex are so scarce—well, that's when half portions like this T. Forsythe Hurd get by as full orders.

Besides, Mrs. Robert had meant well. Her idea was to make the Captain's 48-hour shore leave as gay and lively as possible. She'd had a hard time roundin' up any of his friends, too. Hence Forsythe. One of these slim, fine-haired, well manicured parlor Pomeranians, Forsythe is—the kind who raves over the sandwiches and whispers perfectly killin' things to the ladies as he flits about at afternoon teas.

We were up at the Ellinses', Vee and me, fillin' out at Saturday luncheon, when Mr. Robert drifts in, about an hour behind schedule. You know, he's commandin' one of these coast patrol boats. Some of 'em are converted steam yachts, some are sea-goin' tugs, and then again some are just old menhaden fish-boats painted gray with a few three-inch guns stuck around on 'em casual. And this last is the sort of craft Mr. Robert had wished on him.

Seems there'd been some weather off the Hook for the last few days, and, with a fresh U-boat scare on, him and his reformed glue barge had been havin' anything but a merry time. I don't know how the old fish-boat stood it, but Mr. Robert showed that he'd been on more or less active service. He had a three days' growth of stubble on his face, his navy uniform was wrinkled and brine-stained, and the knuckles on one hand were all barked up.

"Why, Robert!" says young Mrs. Ellins, as she wriggles out of the clinch and gives him the once-over. "You're a sight."

"Sorry, my dear," says Mr. Robert; "but the beauty parlor on the *Narcissus* wasn't working when I left. But if you can give me half an hour to—"

He got it. And when he shows up again in dry togs and with his face mowed he's almost fit to mingle with the guests. It was about then that T. Forsythe was pullin' his star act at the salad bowl. Course, when you have only ordinary people around, you let the kitchen help do such things. But when Forsythe is present he's asked to mix the salad dressin'.

So there is Forsythe, wearin' a jade-green tie to match the color of the salad bowl, surrounded by cruets and pepper grinders and paprika bottles, and manipulatin' his own special olivewood spoon and fork as dainty and graceful as if he was conductin' an orchestra.

"Oh, I say, Jevons," says he, signalin' the Ellinses' butler, "have someone conduct a clove of garlic to the back veranda, slice it, and gently rub it on a crust of fresh bread. Then bring me the bread. And do you mind very much, Mrs. Ellins, if I have those Papa Gontier roses removed? They clash with an otherwise perfect color scheme, and you've no idea how sensitive I am to such jarring notes. Besides, their perfume is so beastly obtrusive. At times I've been made quite ill by them. Really."

"Take them away, Jevons," says Mr. Robert, smotherin' a sarcastic smile.

"Huh!" grumbles Mr. Robert. "What a rotter you are, Forsythe. If I could only get you aboard the *Narcissus* for a ten-day cruise! I'd introduce you to perfumes, the sort you could lean up against. You know, when a boat has carried mature fish for—"

"Please, Bob!" protests Forsythe. "We admit you're a hero, and that you've been saving the country, but don't let's have the disgusting details; at least, not when the salad dressing is at its most critical stage."

Havin' said which, Forsythe proceeds to finish what was for him a hard day's work.

Discussin' his likes and dislikes was Forsythe's strong hold, and, if you could believe him, he had more finicky notions than a sanatorium full of nervous wrecks. He positively couldn't bear the sight of this, the touch of that, and the sound of the other thing. The rustle of a newspaper made him so fidgety he could hardly sit still. The smell of boiled cabbage made him faint. Someone had sent him a plaid necktie for Christmas. He had ordered his man to pick it up with the fire-tongs and throw it in the ash-can. Things like that.

All through luncheon we listened while Forsythe described the awful agonies he'd gone through. We had to listen. You can guess what a joy it was. And, all the time, I could watch Mr. Robert gettin' sorer and sorer.

"Entertainin' party, eh?" I remarks on the side, as we escapes from the dinin'-room.

"Forsythe," says Mr. Robert, "is one of those persons you're always wanting to kick and never do. I could generally avoid him at the club, but here—"

Mr. Robert shrugs his shoulders. Then he adds:

"I say, Torchy, you have clever ideas now and then."

"Who, me?" says I. "Someone's been kiddin' you."

"Perhaps," says he; "but if anything should occur to you that might help toward putting Forsythe in a position where real work and genuine discomfort couldn't be dodged—well, I should be deeply grateful."

"What a cruel thought!" says I. "Still, if a miracle like that could be pulled, it would be entertainin' to watch. Eh?"

"Especially if it had to do with handling cold, slippery things," chuckles Mr. Robert, "like iced eels or pickles."

Then we both grins. I was tryin' to picture Forsythe servin' a sentence as helper in a fish market or assistant stirrer in a soap fact'ry. Not that anything like that could happen through me. Who was I to interfere with a brilliant drawin'-room performer like him? Honest, with Forsythe scintillatin' around, I felt like a Bolsheviki of the third class. And yet, the longer I watched him, the more I mulled over that hint Mr. Robert had thrown out.

I was still wonderin' if I was all hollow above the eyes, when our placid afternoon gatherin' is busted complete by a big cream-colored limousine rollin' through the porte-cochere and a new arrival breezin' in. From the way Jevons swells his chest out as he helps her shed the mink-lined motor coat, I guessed she must be somebody important.

"Why, it's Miss Gorman!" whispers Vee.

"Not *the* Miss Gorman—Miss Jane?" I says.

Vee nods, and I stretches my neck out another kink. Who wouldn't? Not just because she's a society head-liner, or the richest old maid in the country, but because she's such a wonder at gettin' things done. You know, I expect—Red Cross work, suffrage campaignin', Polish relief. Say, I'll bet if she could be turned loose in Mexico or Russia for a couple of months, she'd have things runnin' as smooth as a directors' meetin' of the Standard Oil.

Look at the things she's put through, since the war started, just by crashin' right in and stayin' on the job. They say she keeps four secretaries with their suitcases packed, ready to jump into their travelin' clothes and slide down the pole when she pushes the buzzer button.

And now she's makin' straight for Mr. Robert.

"What luck!" says she. "I wasn't at all sure of finding you. How much leave have you? Only until Monday morning? Oh, you overworked naval officers! But you must find some men for me, Robert; two, at least. I need them at once."

"Might I ask, Miss Jane," says he, "if any particular qualifications are—"

"What I would like," breaks in Miss Gorman, "would be two active, intelligent young men with some initiative and executive ability. You see, I am giving a going away dinner

Sewell Ford

for some soldiers of the Rainbow Division who are about to be sent to the transports. It's an official secret, of course. No one is supposed to know that they are going to sail soon, but everyone does know. None of their friends or relatives are to be allowed to be there to wish them God-speed or anything like that, and they need cheering up just now. So I arrange one of these dinners when I can. My plans for this one, however, have been terribly rushed."

"I see," says Mr. Robert. "And it's perfectly bully of you, Miss Jane. Splendid! I suppose there'll be a hundred or so."

"Six eighty," says she, never battin' an eye. "We are not including the officers—only privates. And we don't want one of them to lift a finger for it. They've had enough fatigue duty. This time they're to be guests—honored guests. I have permission from the Brigadier in command. We are to have one of the mess halls for a whole day. The chef and waiters have been engaged, too. And an orchestra. But there'll be so many to manage—the telling of who to go where, and seeing that the entertainers don't get lost, and that the little dinner favors are put around, and all those details. So I must have help."

I could see Mr. Robert rollin' his eyes around for me, so I steps up. Just from hearin' her talk a couple of minutes I'd caught the fever. That's a way she has, I understand. So the next thing I knew I'd been patted on the shoulder and taken on as a volunteer.

"Precisely the sort of assistant I was hoping for," says Miss Gorman. "I can tell by his hair. I know just what I shall ask him to do. But there'll be so much more; decorating the tables, and—"

Here I nudges Mr. Robert. "How about Forsythe?" I suggests.

"Eh?" says he. "Why—why—By Jove, though! Why not? Oh, I say, Forsythe! Just a moment."

Maybe the same thought struck him as had come to me, which is that helpin' Miss Jane give a blowout to near seven hundred soldiers wouldn't be any rest-cure stunt. She's rated at about ninety horse-power herself, when she's speeded up, and anybody that happens to be on her staff has got to keep movin' in high. They'd have to be ready to tackle anything that turned up, too.

But, to hear Mr. Robert explain it to Forsythe, you'd think it was just that his fame as an arranger of floral center-pieces had spread until Miss Gorman has decided nobody else would do.

"Although, heaven knows, I never suspected you could be really useful, Forsythe," says Mr. Robert. "But if Miss Jane thinks you'd be a help—"

"Oh, I am sure Mr. Hurd would be the very one," puts in Miss Gorman.

"At last!" says Forsythe, strikin' a pose. "My virtues are about to be discovered. I shall be delighted to assist you, Miss Gorman, in any way."

"Tut, tut, Forsythe!" says Mr. Robert. "Don't be too reckless. Miss Jane might take you at your word."

"Go on. Slander me," says Forsythe. "Say that, when enlisted in a noble cause, I am a miserable shirker."

"Indeed, I shouldn't believe a word of it, even if I had time to listen to him," declares Miss Jane. "And I must be at the camp within an hour. I shall need one of you young men now. Let me see. Suppose I take this one—Torchy, isn't it? Get your coat. I'll not promise to have you back for dinner, but I'll try. Thank you so much, Robert."

And then it was a case of goin' on from there. Whew! I've sort of had the notion now and then, when I've been operatin' with Old Hickory Ellins at the Corrugated Trust on busy days, that I was some rapid private sec. But say, havin' followed Miss Jane Gorman through them dinner preliminaries, I know better.

While that French chauffeur of hers is rollin' us down Long Island at from forty to fifty miles per hour, she has her notebook out and is pumpin' me full of things I'm expected to remember—what train the chef's gang is comin' on, how the supplies are to be carted over, who to see about knockin' up a stage for the cabaret talent, and where the buntin' has been ordered. I borrows a pad and pencil, and wishes I knew shorthand.

By the time we lands at the camp, though, I have a fair idea of the job she's tackled; and while she's havin' an interview with the C. O. I starts explorin' the scene of the banquet. First off I finds that the mess-hall seats less than five hundred, the way they got the tables fixed; that there's no room for a stage without breakin' through one end and tackin' it on; and that the camp cooks will have the range ovens full of bread and the tops covered with oatmeal in double boilers as usual. Outside of that and a few other things, the arrangements was lovely.

Miss Jane ain't a bit disturbed when I makes my report.

"There!" says she. "Didn't I say you were just the assistant I needed? Now, please tell all those things to the Brigadier. He will know exactly what to do. Then you'd best be out here early Monday morning to see that they're done properly. And I think, Torchy, I shall make you my general manager for this occasion. Yes, I'll do it. Everyone will report first to you, and you will tell them exactly where to go and what to do."

"You—you mean," says I, gaspin' a bit, "all the hired help?"

"And the volunteers too," says Miss Jane. "Everyone."

Maybe I grinned. I didn't know just how it was goin' to work out, but I could feel something comin'. Forsythe was goin' to get his. He stood to get it good, too. Not all on account of what I owed Mr. Robert for the friendly turns he'd done me. Some of it would be on my own hook, to pay up for the yawny half hours I'd had to sit through listenin' while Forsythe discoursed about himself. You should have seen the satisfied look on Mr. Robert's face when I hinted how Forsythe might be in line for new sensations.

"If I could only be there to watch!" says he. "You must tell me all about it afterwards. They'll enjoy hearing of it at the club."

But, at that, Forsythe wasn't the one to walk right into trouble. He's a shifty party, and he ain't been duckin' work all these years without gettin' expert at it. Accordin' to schedule he was to show up at the camp about nine-thirty Monday morning; but it's nearer noon when he rolls up in his car. And I don't hesitate a bit about givin' him the call.

"You know it's this week, not next," says I, "that this dinner is comin' off. And there's four bolts of buntin' waitin' to be hung up."

"Quite so," says Forsythe. "We must get to work right away."

I had to chase down to the station again then, to see that the chef's outfit was bein' loaded on the trucks; but I was cheered up by the thought of Forsythe balanced on top of a tall step-ladder with his mouth full of tacks and his collar gettin' wilty.

It's near an hour before I gets back, though. Do I find Forsythe in his shirt-sleeves climbin' around on the rafters? I do not. He's sittin' comfortable in a camp-chair on a fur motor robe, smokin' a cigarette calm, and surrounded by half a dozen classy young ladies that he's rounded up by 'phone from the nearest country club. The girls and three or four chauffeurs are doin' the work, while Forsythe is doin' the heavy directin'.

He'd sketched out his decoratin' scheme on the back of an envelop, and now he was tellin' 'em how to carry it out. The worst of it is, too, that he's gettin' some stunnin' effects and is bein' congratulated enthusiastic by the girls.

It's the same way with fixin' up the tables with ferns and flowers. Forsythe plans it out with a pencil, and his crew do the hustlin' around.

Course, I had to let it ride. Besides, there was a dozen other things for me to look after. But I'm good at a waitin' game. I kept my eye on Forsythe, to see that he didn't slip away. He was still there at two-thirty, havin' organized a picnic luncheon with the young ladies, when Miss Jane blew in. And blamed if she don't fall for Forsythe's stuff, too.

"Why, you've done wonders, Mr. Hurd," says she. "What a versatile genius you are?"

"Oh, that!" says he, wavin' a sandwich careless. "But it's an inspiration to be doing anything at all for you, Miss Gorman."

And here he hasn't so much as shed his overcoat.

It must have been half an hour later when Sig. Zaretti, the head chef, comes huntin' me out with a desperate look in his eyes. I was consultin' Miss Jane about borrowin' a piano from the Y. M. C. A. tent, but he kicks right in.

"Ah, I am distract," says he, puffin' out his cheeks. "Eet—eet ees too mooch!"

"Go on," says I. "Shoot the tragedy. What's too much?"

"That Pedro and that Salvatore," says he. "They have become lost, the worthless ones. They disappear on me. And in three hours I am to serve, in this crude place, a dinner of six courses to seven hundred men. They abandon me at such a time, with so much to be done."

"Well, that's up to you," says I. "Can't some of your crowd double in brass? What about workin' in some of your waiters?"

"But they are all employed," says Zaretti. "Besides, the union does not permit. If you could assist me with two men, even one. I implore."

"There ain't a cook in sight," says I. "Sorry, but—"

"Eet ees not for cook," he protests. "No; only to help make the peel from those so many potatoes. One who could make the peel. Please!"

"Oh!" says I. "Peelin' potatoes! Why, 'most anybody could help out at that, I guess. I would myself if—"

"No," breaks in Miss Jane. "You cannot be spared. And I'm

sure I don't know who could."

"Unless," I puts in, "Mr. Hurd is all through with his decoratin'."

"Why, to be sure," says she. "Just tell him, will you?"

"Suppose I send him over to you, Miss Gorman," says I, "while I hustle along that piano?"

She nods, and I lose no time trailin' down Forsythe.

"Emergency call for you from Miss Jane," says I, edgin' in among his admirers and tappin' him on the shoulder. "She's waitin' over by headquarters."

"Oh, certainly," says Forsythe, startin' off brisk.

"And say," I calls after him, "I hope it won't be anything that'll make you faint."

"Please don't worry about me," says he.

Well, I tried not to. In fact, I tried so hard that some folks might have thought I'd heard good news from home. But I'd had a peek or two into the camp kitchen since Zaretti's food construction squad had moved in, and, believe me, it was no place for an artistic temperament, subject to creeps up the back. There was about a ton of cold-storage turkeys bein' unpacked, bushels of onions goin' through the shuckin' process, buckets of soup stock standin' around, and half a dozen murderous-lookin' assistant chefs was sharpenin' long knives and jabberin' excited in four languages.

Oh, yes; Forsythe was goin' to need all the inspiration he'd collected, if he lasted through.

I kind of wanted to stick around and cheer him up with friendly words while he was fishin' potatoes out of the cold water and learnin' to use a peelin'-knife, but my job wouldn't let me. After I'd seen the piano landed on the new stage, there were chairs to be placed for the orchestra, and then other things. So it was some little time before I got around to the kitchen wing again, pretendin' to be lookin' for Zaretti. But nowhere in that steamin', hustlin', garlic-smellin' bunch could I see Forsythe.

"Hey, chef!" I sings out. "Where's that expert potato-peeler I sent you?"

"Ah!" says he, rubbin' his hands enthusiastic. "The signor with the yellow gloves? In the tent there you will find heem."

So I steps over to the door of a sort of canvas annex and peers in. And say, it was a rude shock. Forsythe is there, all right. He's snuggled up cozy next to an oil heater, holdin' a watch in one hand and a cigarette in the other, while around him is grouped his faithful fluff body-guard, each with a pan in her lap and the potato-peelin's comin' off rapid. Forsythe? Oh, he seems to be speedin' 'em up and keepin' tally.

I'd just let out my second gasp when I feels somebody at my elbow, and glances round to find it's Miss Jane.

"Look!" says I, indicatin' Forsythe and his busy bees.

"What a picture!" says Miss Jane.

"Yes," says I, "illustratin' the manly art of lettin' the women do it."

Miss Jane laughs easy.

"It has been that way for ages," says she. "Mr. Hurd is only running true to type. But see! The potatoes are nearly all peeled and our dinner is going to be served on time. What splendid assistants you've both been!"

At that, though, if there'd been a medal to be passed out, I guess it would have been pinned on Forsythe.

CHAPTER XV

THE HOUSE OF TORCHY

This trip it was a matter of tanks. No, not the ice-water variety, or the kind that absorbs high-balls. Army tanks—the sort that wallows out at daybreak and gives the Hun that chilly feelin' down his spine.

Accordin' to my credentials, I was supposed to be inspectin' 'em for weak spots in the armor or punk work on the gears. And I can tell you now, on the side, that it was 90 per cent. bluff. What the Ordnance Department really wanted to know was whether the work was bein' speeded up proper, how many men on the shifts, and was the steel comin' through from the rollin' mills all right. Get me? Sleuth stuff.

I'd been knockin' around there for four days, bein' towed about by the reserve major, who had a face on him like a stuffed owl, a nut full of decimal fractions, and a rubber-stamp mind. Oh, he was on the job, all right. So was everybody else in sight. I could see that after the first day. In fact, I coded in my O. K. the second noon and was plannin' to slip back home.

But when I hinted as much to the Major he nearly threw a cat-fit. Why, he'd arranged a demonstration at 10 A.M.

Thursday, for my special benefit. And there were the tests—horse-power, gun-ranges, resistance, and I don't know what all; technical junk that I savvied about as much as if he'd been tryin' to show me how to play the Chinese alphabet on a piccolo.

Course, I couldn't tell him that, nor I didn't want to break his heart by refusin'. So I agrees to stick around a while longer. But say, I never enjoyed such a poor time doin' it. For there was just one spot on the map where I was anxious to be for the next few days. That was at home. It was one of the times when I ought to be there too, for—Well, I'll get to that later.

Besides, this fact'ry joint where they were buildin' the tanks wasn't any allurin' spot. I can't advertise just where it was, either; the government wouldn't like it. But if there's any part of Connecticut that's less interestin' to loaf around in, I never got stranded there. You run a spur track out into the bare hills for fifteen miles from nowhere, slap up a row of cement barracks, and a few acres of machine shops, string a ten-foot barbed-wire fence around the plant, drape the whole outfit in soft-coal smoke, and you ain't got any Garden of Eden winter resort. Specially when it's full of low-brow mechanics who speak in seven different lingos and subsist mainly on cut plug and garlic.

After I'd checked up all the dope I'd come for, and durin' the times when the Major was out plannin' more inspection stunts for me, I was left to drill around by myself. Hours and hours. And all there was to read in the Major's office was engineerin' magazines and the hist'ry of Essex County, Mass. Havin' been fed up on mechanics, I tackled the hist'ry. One chapter had a corkin' good Indian scalpin' story in it, about a Mrs. Hannah Dustin; and say, as a short-order hair remover she was a lady champ, all right. But the rest of the book wasn't so thrillin'.

So I tried chattin' with the Major's secretary, a Lieutenant Barnes. The Major must have picked him out on account of that serious face of his. First off, I had an idea Barnes was sad just because he was detailed at this soggy place instead of bein' sent to France. I asks him sort of sympathizin' how long he's been here. He says three months.

"In this hole?" says I. "How do you keep from goin' bughouse?"

"I don't mind it," says he. "I find the work quite interesting."

"But evenin's?" I suggests.

"I write to my wife," says he.

I wanted to ask him what about, but I choked it back. "Oh, yes," says I. "Of course. Any youngsters at home!"

"No," says he prompt. "Life is complicated enough without children."

"Oh, I don't know," says I. "They'd sort of help, I should think."

He shakes his head and glares gloomy out of the window. "I cannot agree with you," says he. "Perhaps you have never seriously considered just what it means to be a parent."

"Maybe not," says I, "but—"

"Few seem to do so," he breaks in. "Just think: one begins by putting two lives in jeopardy."

"Let's pass over that," I says hasty.

He sighs. "If we only could," says he. "And then—Well, there you are—saddled with the task of caring for another human being, of keeping him in good health, of molding his character, of planning and directing his whole career, from boyhood on."

"Some are girls, though," I suggests.

He shudders. "So much the worse," says he. "Girl babies are such delicate creatures; all babies are, in fact. Do you know the average rate of infant mortality in this country? Just think of the hundreds of thousands who do not survive the teething period. Imagine the anxieties, the sleepless nights, the sad little tragedies which come to so many homes. Then the epidemic diseases—measles, scarlet fever, meningitis. Let them survive all those, and what has the parent to face but the battle with other plagues, mental and moral? Think of the number of weak-minded children there are in the world; of perverts, criminally inclined. It is staggering. But if you escape all that, if your children are well and normal, as some are, then you must consider this: Suppose anything should happen to either or both of the parents? What of the little boy or girl? You have seen orphan asylums, I suppose. Have you ever stopped to—"

And then, just as he had me feelin' like I ought to be led out and shot at sunrise, the old Major comes bustlin' in fussy. I could have fallen on his neck.

"All ready!" says he. "Now I'll show you a fighting machine, young man, that is the last word in mechanical genius."

"You can show me anything, Major," says I, "so long as it ain't a morgue or a State's prison."

And he sure had some boiler-plate bus out there champin' at

the bit. It looked just as frisky as the Flatiron Buildin', squattin' in the middle of the field, this young Fort Slocum with the caterpillar wheels sunk in the mud.

"Stuck, ain't she?" I asked the Major.

"We shall see," says he, noddin' to one of his staff, who proceeds to do a semaphore act with his arms.

An answerin' snort comes from inside the thing, a purry sort of rumble that grows bigger and bigger, and next I knew, it starts wallowin' right at us. It keeps comin' and comin', gettin' up speed all the while, and if there hadn't been a four-foot stone wall between us I'd been lookin' for a tall tree. I thought it would turn when it came to the wall. But it don't. It gives a lurch, like a cow playin' leap-frog, and over she comes, still pointed our way.

"Hey, Major!" I calls out above the roar. "Can they see where they're goin' in there? Hadn't we better give 'em room?"

"Don't move, please," says he.

"Just as you say," says I; "only I ain't strong for bein' rolled into pie-crust."

"There's no danger," says he. "I merely wish you to see how—There! Look!"

And say, within twenty feet of us the blamed thing rears up on its haunches, its ugly nose high as a house above us, and, while I'm still holdin' my breath, it pivots on its tail and lumbers back, leavin' a path that looks like it had been paved with Belgian blocks.

Course, that's only part of the performance. We watched it wallow into deep ditches and out, splash through a brook, and mow down trees more'n a foot thick. And all the time the crew were pokin' out wicked-lookin' guns, big and little, that swung round and hunted us out like so many murderous eyes.

"Cute little beast, ain't it?" says I. "You got it trained so it'll almost do a waltz. If I was to pick my position, though, I think I'd rather be on the inside lookin' out."

"Very well," says the Major. "You shall have a ride in it."

"Excuse me," says I. "I was only foolin'. Honest, Major, I ain't yearnin'."

"Telegram for you," breaks in Barnes, the secretary.

"Oh!" says I, a bit gaspy, as I rips open the envelop.

It's the one I'd been espectin'. All it says is: "Come at once. VEE." But I knew what that meant.

"Sorry, Major," says I, "but I'll have to pass up the rest of the show. I—I'm called back."

"Ah! To headquarters?" says he.

"No," says I. "Home."

He shakes his head and frowns. "That is a word which no officer is supposed to have in his vocabulary," says he.

"It's in mine, all right," says I. "But then, I'm not much of an army officer, anyway. I'm mostly a camouflaged private sec. Besides, this ain't any ordinary call. It's a domestic S. O. S.

that I've been sort of lookin' for."

"I understand," says he. "The—the first?"

I nods. Then I asks: "What's the quickest way across to Long Island?"

"There isn't any quick way," says he, "unless you have wings. You can't even catch the branch line local that connects with the New York express now. There'll be one down at 8:36 to-morrow morning, though."

"Wha-a-at!" says I, gawpin' at him. "How about gettin' a machine and shootin' down to the junction?"

"My car is the only one here," says he, "and that is out of commission to-day—valves being ground."

"But look," says I; "you got three or four of those motor-cycles with a bath-tub tacked on the side. Couldn't you let one of your sergeants—"

"Strictly against orders," says he, "except for military purposes."

"Ah, stretch it, Major," I goes on. "Have a heart. Just think! I want to get there to-night. Got to!"

"Impossible," says he.

"But listen—" I keeps on.

Well, it's no use rehearsin' the swell arguments I put up. I said he had a rubber-stamp mind, didn't I? And I made about as much headway talkin' to him as I would if I'd been assaultin' that tank with a tack-hammer. He couldn't see any difference between havin' charge of a string of machine shops in Connecticut and commandin' a regiment in the front-line trenches. Besides, he didn't approve of junior officers bein' married. Not durin' war-time, anyway.

And the worst of it was, I couldn't tell him just the particular kind of ossified old pinhead I thought he was. All I could do was grind my teeth, say "Yes, sir," and salute respectful.

Also there was that undertaker-faced secretary standin' by with his ear out. The prospect of sittin' around watchin' him for the rest of the day wasn't fascinatin'. No; I'd had about all of Barnes I could stand. A few more of his cheerin' observations, and I'd want to jam his head into his typewriter and then tread on the keys. Nor I wasn't goin' to be fed on any more cog-wheel statistics by the Major, either.

All I could keep on my mind then was this one thing: How could I get home? Looked like I was up against it, too. The nearest town was twelve miles off, and the main-line junction was some thirty-odd miles beyond that. Too far for an afternoon hike. But I couldn't just sit around and wait, or pace up and down inside the barbed-wire fence like an enemy alien that had been pastured out. So I wanders through the gate and down a road. I didn't know where it led, or care. Maybe I had a vague idea a car would come along. But none did.

I must have been trampin' near an hour, with my chin down and my fists jammed into my overcoat pockets, when I catches a glimpse, out of the tail of my eye, of something yellow dodgin' behind a clump of cedars at one side of the road. First off I thought it might be a cow, as there was a farm-house a little ways ahead. Then it struck me no cow would move as quick as that, or have such a bright yellow hide. So I turns and makes straight for the cedars.

It was a thick, bushy clump. I climbed the stone wall and walked all the way round. Nothin' in sight. Seemed as if I could see branches movin' in there, though, and hear a sound like heavy breathin'. Course, it might be a deer, or a fox. Then I remembered I had half a bag of peanuts somewhere about me. Maybe I could toll the thing out with 'em. I was just fishin' in my pockets when from the middle of the cedars comes this disgusted protest.

"Oh, I say, old man," says a voice. "No shooting, please."

And with that out steps a clean-cut, cheerful-faced young gent in a leather coat, goggled helmet, and spiral puttees. No wonder I stood starin'. Not that I hadn't seen plenty like him before, but I didn't know the woods was so full of 'em.

"You were out looking for me, I suppose?" he goes on.

"Depends on who you are," says I.

"Oh, we might as well come down to cases," says he. "I'm the enemy."

"You don't look it," says I, grinnin'.

He shrugs his shoulders.

"Fact, old man," says he. "I'm the one you were sent to watch for—Lieutenant Donald Allen, 26th Flying Corps Division, Squadron B."

"Pleased to meet you," says I.

"No doubt," says he. "Have a cigarette?" We lights up from the same match. "But say," he adds, "it was just a piece of tough luck, your catching me in this fix."

"Oh, I ain't so sure," says I.

"Of course," he says, "it won't go with the C. O. But really, now, what are you going to do when your observer insists that he's dying? I couldn't tell. Perhaps he was. Right in the middle of a perfect flight, too, the chump! Motor working sweet, air as smooth as silk, and no cross currents to speak of. But, with him howling about this awful pain in his tummy, what else could I do? Had to come down and—Well, here we are. I'm behind the lines, I suppose, and you'll report my surrender."

"Then what?" I asks.

"Oh," says Allen, "as soon as I persuade this trolley-car aviator, Martin, that he isn't dead, I shall load him into the old bus and cart him back to Mineola."

"Wha-a-t!" says I. "You—you're goin' back to Mineola—to-night?"

"If Martin can forget his tummy," says he. "How I'll be guyed! Go to the foot of the eligible list too, and probably miss out on being sent over with my division. Oh, well!"

I was beginning to dope out the mystery. More'n that, I had my fingers on the tail feathers of a hunch.

"Why not leave Martin here?" I suggests. "Couldn't you show up in time?"

"It wouldn't count," says the Lieutenant. "You must have an observer all the way."

"How about me subbin' in?" says I.

"You?" says he. "Why, you're on the other side."

"That's where you're mixed," says I. "I'm on the wrong side of Long Island Sound, that's all."

"Why," says he, "weren't you sent out to—"

"No," I breaks in; "I'm no spotter. I'm on special detail from the Ordnance Department. And a mighty punk detail at that, if you ask me. The party who's sleuthin' for you, I expect, is the one I saw back at the plant, moonin' around with a pair of field glasses strapped to him. You ain't captured yet; not by me, anyway."

"Honest?" says he. "Why, then—then—"

"Uh-huh!" says I. "And if you can make it back to Mineola with a perfectly good passenger in the extra seat you'll qualify for scout work and most likely be over pluggin' Huns within a month or so. That won't tickle you a bit more'n it will me to get to Long Island to-night, for—"

Well, then I tells him about Vee, and everything.

"By George!" says he. "You're all right, Lieutenant—er—"

"Ah, between friends, Donald," says I, "it's Torchy."

At which we links arms chummy and goes marchin' close order down to the farm-house to see how this Martin party was gettin' on. We finds him rolled up in quilts on an old sofa that the folks had shoved up in front of the stove—a slim, nervous-lookin' young gink with sandy hair and a peaked nose.

"Well, how about you?" asks Allen.

Martin he only moans and reaches for a warm flat-iron that he'd been holdin' against his stomach.

"Still dying, eh?" says Allen. "Why didn't you report sick this morning, instead of letting them send you up with me?"

"I—I was all right then," whines Martin. "It—it must have been the altitude got me. I—I'd never been that high before, you know."

"Bah!" says the Lieutenant. "Not over thirty-five hundred at any time. How do you expect me to take you back—on the hundred-foot level? You'll make a fine observer, you will!"

"I've had enough observing," says Martin. "I—I'm going to get transferred to the mechanical department."

"Oh, are you?" says Allen. "Then you'll be just as satisfied to make the trip back by rail."

Martin nods.

"And you won't be needing your helmet and things, eh?" goes on the Lieutenant. "I'll take those along, then," and he winks at me.

All of a sudden, though, the sparkles fade out of his eyes. "Jinxed again!" says he. "There'd be no blessed map to hand in."

"Eh?" says I. "Map of what!"

He explains jerky. This scoutin' stunt of his was to locate the tank works and get close enough for an observer to draw a plan of it—all of which he'd done, only by then Martin had got past the drawin' stage.

"So it's no use going back to-night."

"Ain't it?" says I. "Say, if a map of that smoky hole is all you need, I guess I can produce that easy enough."

"Can you?" he asks.

"Why not?" says I. "Ain't I been cooped up there for nearly a week? I can put in a bird's-eye view of the Major in command; one of his secretary, too, if you like. Gimme some paper."

And inside of five minutes I'd sketched out a diagram of the buildin's and the whole outfit. Then we poked Martin up long enough for him to sign it.

"Fine work!" says Donald. "That earns you a hop, all right. Now buckle yourself into that cloud costume and I'll show you how a 110-horse-power crow would go from here to the middle of Long Island if he was in a hurry."

"You can't make it any too speedy for me," says I, slippin' into the sheepskin jacket.

"Ever been up before?" he asks.

"Only once—in a hydro," says I; "but I ain't missed any chances."

"That's the spirit!" says he. "Come along. The old bus is anchored down the field a ways."

I couldn't hardly believe I was actually goin' to pull it off until he'd got the motor started and we went skimmin' along the ground. But as soon as we shook off the State of Connecticut and began climbin' up over a strip of woods, I settles back in the little cockpit, buttons the wind-shield over my mouth, and sighs contented.

Allen and I didn't exchange much chat. You don't with an engine of that size roarin' a few feet in front of you and your ears buttoned down by three or four layers of wool and leather. Once he points out ahead and tries to shout something, I don't know what. But I nods and waves encouragin'. Later he points down and grins. I grins back.

Next thing I knew, he's shut off the motor, and I gets a glimpse of the whole of Long Island behavin' odd. Seems as if it's swellin' and widenin' out, like one of these freaky toy balloons you blow up. It didn't seem as if we was divin' down—more like the map was rushin' up to meet us. Pretty soon I could make out a big open space with a lot of squatty buildin's at one end, and in a couple of minutes more the machine was rollin' along on its wheels and we taxied graceful up towards the hangars.

It was just gettin' dusk as we piles out, and the first few yards I walked I felt like I was dressed in a divin' suit with a pair of lead boots on my feet. I saw Allen salute an officer, hand over the map, and heard him say something about Observer Martin wantin' to report sick. Then he steers me off toward the barracks, circles past' em, and leads me through a back gate.

"I think we've put it over, old man," says he, givin' me the cordial grip. "I can't tell you what a good turn you've done me."

"It's fifty-fifty," says I. "Where do I hit a station?"

"You take this trolley that's coming," says he. "That junk you have on you can send back to-morrow, in my care. And I—I trust you'll find things all right at home."

"Thanks," says I. "Hope you'll have the same luck yourself some day."

"Oh, perhaps," says he, shakin' his head doubtful. "If I ever get back. But not until I'm past thirty, anyway."

"Why so late?" asks I.

"What would get my goat," says he, "would be the risk of breakin' into the grandfather class before I got ready."

"Gee!" I gasps. "I hadn't thought of that."

So, with this new idea, and the cheerin' views Barnes had pumped into me, I has plenty to chew over durin' the next hour or so that I'm speedin' towards home. I expect that accounts some for the long face I must have been wearin' when I finally dashes through the front gate of the Lilacs and am let into the house by Leon Battou, the little old Frenchman who cooks and buttles for us.

"Ah, *mon Dieu!*" says Leon, throwin' up his hands and starin' at me bug-eyed. "Monsieur!"

"Go on," says I. "Tell me the worst. What is it?"

"But no, M'sieur," says he. "It is only that M'sieur appears in so strange attire."

"Oh! These?" says I. "Never mind my costume, Leon. What about Vee?"

"Ah!" says he, his eyes beamin' once more and his hands washin' each other. "Madame is excellent. She herself will tell you. Come!"

Upstairs I went, two steps at a time.

"S-s-sh!" says the nurse, meetin' me at the door.

But I brushes past her, and the next minute I'm over by the bed and Vee is smilin' up at me. It's only the ghost of a smile, but it means a lot to me. She slips one of her hands into mine.

"Torchy," she whispers, "did you drop down out of—of the air?"

"That was about it," says I. "I got here, though. Are you all right, girlie?"

She nods and gives me another of them sketchy, happy smiles.

"And how about the—the—" I starts to ask.

She glances towards the corner where the nurse is bendin' over a pink and white basket. "He's splendid," she whispers.

"He?" says I. "Then—then it's a boy?"

She gives my hand a little squeeze.

And ten minutes later, when I'm shooed out, I'm feelin' so chesty and happy that I'm tingly all over.

Down in the livin'-room Leon is waitin' for me, wearin' a broad grin. He greets me with his hand out. And then, somehow, because he's so different, I expect, I remembers Barnes. I was wonderin' if Leon was just puttin' on.

"Well," says I, "how about it?"

"Ah, Monsieur!" says he, givin' me the hearty grip. "I make to you my best congratulations."

"Then you don't feel," says I, "that bein' a parent is kind of a sad and solemn business?"

"Sad!" says he. "*Non, non!* It is the grand joy of life. It is when you have the best right to be proud and glad, for to you has come *la bonne chance*. Yes, *la bonne chance!*"

And say, there's no mistakin' that Leon means every word of it, French and all.

"Thanks, Leon," says I. "You ought to know. You've been through it yourself. I'll bet you wouldn't even feel bad at being a grandfather. No? Well, I guess I'll follow through on that line. Maybe I don't deserve so much luck, but I'm takin' it just as though I did. And say, Leon, let's us go out in the back yard and give three cheers for the son and heir of the house of Torchy."

CHAPTER XVI

TORCHY GETS THE THUMB GRIP

I expect a lot of people thought it about me; but the one who really registered the idea was Auntie. Trust her. For of course, with an event of this kind staged in the house we couldn't expect to dodge a visit from the old girl. She came clear up from Miami—although, with so much trouble about through sleepers and everything, I kept tellin' Vee I was afraid she wouldn't think it worth while makin' the trip.

"How absurd, Torchy!" says Vee. "Not want to see baby? To be sure, she will."

You see, Vee had the right hunch from the very first—about the importance of this new member of the fam'ly, I mean. She took it as a matter of course that everybody who'd ever known or heard of us would be anxious to rush in and gaze awe-struck and reverent at this remarkable addition we'd made to the population of Long Island. Something like that. She don't have to work up to it. Seems to come natural. Why, say, she'd sit by and listen without crackin' a smile to these regular gushers who laid it on so thick you'd 'most thought the youngster himself would have turned over and run his tongue out at 'em.

"Oh, the dear, darling 'ittle cherub!" they'd squeal. "Isn't he simp-ly the most won-der-ful baby you ev-er saw?"

And Vee would never blink an eye. In fact, she'd beam on 'em grateful, and repeat to me afterwards what they'd said, like it was just a case of the vote bein' made unanimous, as she knew it was bound to be all along.

Which wasn't a bit like any of the forty-seven varieties of Vee I thought I was so well acquainted with. No. I'll admit she'd shown whims and queer streaks now and then, and maybe a fault or so; but nothing that had anything to do with any tendency of the ego to stick its elbows out. Yet, when it comes to listenin' to flatterin' remarks about our son and heir—well, no Broadway star readin' over what his press-agent had smuggled into the dramatic notes had anything on her. She couldn't have it handed to her too strong.

As for me, I guess I was in sort of a daze there for a week or so. Gettin' to be a parent had been sprung on me so sudden that it was sort of confusin'. I couldn't let on to be a judge of babies myself. I don't know as I'd ever examined one real near to before, anyway—not such a new one as this.

And, between me and you, when I did get a chance to size him up real close once,—they'd all gone out of the room and left me standin' by the crib,—I was kind of disappointed. Uh-huh. No use kiddin' yourself. I couldn't see a thing wonderful about him, or where he was much different from others I'd glanced at casual. Such a small party to have so much fuss made over! Why, one of his hands wasn't much bigger'n a cat's paw. And his face was so red and little and the nose so sketchy that it didn't seem likely he'd ever amount to much. Here he'd had more'n a week to grow in, and I couldn't notice any change at all.

Not that I was nutty enough to report any such thoughts. Hardly. I felt kind of guilty at just havin' 'em in my head. How was it, I asked myself, that I couldn't stand around with my hands clasped and my eyes dimmed up, as a perfectly good parent should when he gazes at his first and only chee-ild! Wasn't I human?

All the alibi I can put up is that I wasn't used to bein' a father. Ain't there something in that? Just think, now. Why, I'd hardly got used to bein' married. Here, only a little over a year ago, I was floatin' around free and careless. And then, first thing I know, without any special coachin' in the act, I finds myself pushed out into the center of the stage with the spot-light on me, and I'm introduced as a daddy.

The only thing I could do was try to make a noise like one. I didn't feel it, any more'n I felt like a stained-glass saint in a church window. And I didn't know the lines very well. But there was everybody watching,—Vee, and the nurse, and Madame Battou, and occasional callers,—so I proceeds to bluff it through the best I could.

My merry little idea was to be familiar with the youngster, treat him as if he'd been a member of the fam'ly for a long time, and hide any embarrassin' feelin's I might have by addressin' him loud and joshin'. I expect it was kind of a poor performance, at that. But I seemed to be gettin' away with it, so I stuck to that line. Vee appears to take it all right, and, as nobody else gave me the call, I almost got to believe it was the real thing myself.

So this particular afternoon, when I came breezin' in from town, I chases right up to the nursery, where I knew I'd find Vee, gives her the usual hail just behind the ear, and then turns hasty to the crib to show I haven't forgot who's there.

"Hello, old sport!" says I, ticklin' him in the ribs. "How you hittin' 'em, hey? Well, well! Look at the fistses doubled up! Who you goin' to hand a wallop to now? Oh, tryin' to punch yourself in the eye, are you? Come there, you young rough-houser, lay off that grouchy stuff and speak some kind words to your daddy. You won't, eh? Goin' to kick a little with the footsies. That's it. Mix in with all fours, you young—"

And just then I hears a suppressed snort that sounds sort of familiar. I glances around panicky, and gets the full benefit of a disgusted glare from a set of chilled steel eyes, and discovers that there's someone besides Vee and the nurse present. Yep. It's Auntie.

"May I ask," says she, "if this is your usual manner of greeting your offspring?"

"Why," says I, "I—I expect it is."

"Humph!" says she. "I might have known."

"Now, Auntie," protests Vee, "you know very well that Torchy means—"

"Whatever he means or doesn't mean," breaks in Auntie, "I am sure he has an astonishing way of showing parental affection. Calling the child an 'old scout,' a 'young rough-houser'! It's shocking."

"Sorry," says I; "but I ain't taken any lessons in polite baby talk yet. Maybe in time I could learn this ittums-tweetums stuff, but I doubt it. Always made me sick, that did; and one of the things Vee and I agreed on was that—"

"Oh, very well," says Auntie. "I do not intend to interfere in any way."

As if she could help it! Why, say, she'd give St. Peter advice on gate-keepin'. But for the time bein', each of us havin' had our say, we calls it a draw and gets back to what looks like a peace footin'. But from then on I knew she had her eyes out at me. Every move I made was liable to get her breathin' short or set her squirmin' in her chair. And you know how it's apt to be in a case like that. I made more breaks than ever. I'd forget about the youngster bein' asleep and cut loose with something noisy at the wrong time. Or I'd jolt her some other way.

But she held in until, one night after dinner, when the baby had indulged in too much day sleepin' and was carryin' on a bit, I takes a notion to soothe him with a few humorous antics while Auntie is safe downstairs. You see, I'd never been able to get him to take any notice of me before; but this time, after I'd done a swell imitation of a Fred Stone dance, I had him cooin' approvin', the nurse smotherin' a smile, and Vee snickerin'.

Naturally, I has to follow it up with something else. I was down on my hands and knees doin' a buckin' bronco act across the floor, when there comes this gasp from the doorway. It seems Auntie was passin' by, and peeked in. Her eyebrows go up, her mouth corners come down, and she stiffens like she'd grabbed a high-voltage feed wire. I saw it comin', but the best I can do is steady myself on my fingers and toes and wish I had cotton in my ears.

"Really!" says she. "Are you never to realize, young man, that you are now supposed to be a husband and a father?"

And, before I can shoot back a word, she's sailed on, her chin in the air and her mouth about as smilin' as a crack in a vinegar bottle. But she'd said it. She'd pushed it home, too. And the worst of it was, I couldn't deny that she had the goods on me. I might pass as a husband, if you didn't expect too much. But as for the rest—well, I knew I wasn't meetin' the specifications.

The only model I could think of was them fond parent groups you see in the movie close-ups—mother on the right, father at the left, and Little Bright Eyes squeezed in between and bein' mauled affectionate. Had we ever indulged in any such family clinch? Not up to date. Why? Was it because I was a failure as a daddy? Looked so. And here was Auntie taxin' me with it. Would other folks find out, too?

I begun thinkin' over the way different ones had taken the news. Old Hickory, for instance. I was wearin' a wide grin and still feelin' sort of chesty when I broke into his private office and handed him the bulletin.

"Eh?" he grunts, squintin' at me from under them bushy eyebrows. "A father! You? Good Lord!"

"Why not?" says I. "It's still being done, ain't it?"

"Oh, I suppose so. Yes, yes," he goes on, starin' at me. "But somehow, young man, I can hardly think of you as—as— Well, congratulations, Torchy. You have frequently surprised me by rising to the occasion. Perhaps you will in this also."

"Thanks, Mr. Ellins," says I. "It's nice of you to cheer me up that way."

Piddie, of course, said the right and elegant thing, just as if he'd learned it out of a book. He always does, you know. Makes a reg'lar little speech, and finishes by givin' me the fraternal handclasp and a pat on the shoulder.

But a minute after I caught him gazin' at me wonderin', and he goes off shakin' his head.

Then I runs across my newspaper friend Whitey Weeks, who used to know me when I was a cub office-boy on the Sunday editor's door.

"Well, Torchy," says he, "what you got on your mind?"

"Nothing you could make copy out of," says I, "but it's a whale of an event for me."

"You don't say," says he. "Somebody died and left you the business?"

"Just the opposite," says I.

"I don't get you," says he.

"Ah, what's usually in the next column?" says I. "It's a case of somebody bein' born."

"Why—why," says he, openin' his mouth, "you don't mean that—"

"Uh-huh," says I, tryin' to look modest.

"Haw-haw!" roars Whitey, usin' the steam siren effect. And, as it's right on the corner of Forty-second and Broadway, he comes near collectin' a crowd. Four or five people turn around to see what the merriment is all about, and a couple of 'em stops short in their tracks. One guy I spotted for a vaudeville artist lookin' for stuff that might fat up his act.

"Say," Whitey goes on, poundin' me on the back jovial, "that's rich, that is!"

"Glad it amuses you," says I, startin' to move off.

"Oh, come, old chap!" says he, followin' along. "Don't get crabby. What—what is it, anyway?"

"It's a baby," says I. "Quite a young one. Now go laugh your fat head off, you human hyena."

With that shot I dashes through the traffic and catches a downtown car, leavin' him there with his silly face unhinged. And I did no more announcin' to anybody. I was through advertisin'. When some of the commuters on the eight-three heard the news and started springin' their comic tricks on me, I pretended I didn't understand.

I don't know what they thought. I didn't give a whoop, either. I wasn't demandin' that anybody should pass solemn resolutions thankin' me for what I'd done for my country, or stand with their hats off as I went by. But I was overstocked on this joke-book junk.

Maybe I didn't look like a father, or act like one; but I was doin' my best on the short notice I'd had.

I will say for Vee that she stood by me noble. She seemed to think whatever I did was all right, even when I shied at holdin' the youngster for the first time.

"I'm afraid I'll bend him in the wrong place," I protests.

"Goose!" says she. "Of course you won't."

"Suppose I should drop him?" says I.

"You can't if you take him just as I show you," she goes on patient. "Now, sit down in that chair. Crook your left arm like this. Now hold your knees together, and we'll just put the little precious right in your—There! Why, you're doing it splendidly."

"Am I?" says I.

I might have believed her if I hadn't caught a glimpse of myself in the glass. Say, I was sittin' there as easy and graceful as if I'd been made of structural iron and reinforced concrete. Stiff! Them stone lions in front of the Public Lib'ry was frolicsome lambs compared to me. And I was wearin' the same happy look on my face as if I was havin' a tooth plugged.

Course that had to be just the time when Mr. Robert Ellins happened in for his first private view. Mrs. Robert had towed him down special. He's a reg'lar friend, though, Mr. Robert is. I can't say how much of a struggle he had to keep his face straight, but after the first spasm has worn off he don't show any more signs of wantin' to cackle. And he don't pull any end-man stuff.

"Well, well, Torchy!" says he. "A son and heir, eh? I salute you."

"Same to you and many of 'em," says I, grinnin' simple.

It was the first thing that came into my head, but I guess I'd better not have let it out. Mrs. Robert pinks up, Vee snickers, and they both hurries into the next room.

"Thank you, Torchy," says Mr. Robert. "Within certain limitations, I trust your wish comes true. But I say—how does it feel, being a father?"

"Just plain foolish," says I.

"Eh?" says he.

"Honest, Mr. Robert," says I, "I never felt so much like a ham sandwich at a Chamber of Commerce banquet as I do right now. I'm beginnin' to suspect I've been miscast for the part."

"Nonsense!" says he soothin'. "You appear to be getting along swimmingly. I'm sure I wouldn't know how to hold a baby at all."

"You couldn't know less'n I do about it at present writing," says I. "I don't dare move, and both my legs are asleep from the knees down. Do me a favor and call for help, won't you?"

"Oh, I say!" he calls out. "The starboard watch wants to be relieved."

So Vee comes back and pries the baby out of my grip.

"Isn't he absurd!" says she. "But he will soon learn. All men are like that at first, I suppose."

"Hear that, Mr. Robert?" says I. "That's what I call a sun-cured disposition."

She'd make a good animal-trainer, Vee; she's so persistent and patient. After dinner she jollies me into tryin' it again.

"You needn't sit so rigid, you know," she coaches me. "Just relax naturally and let his little head rest easy in the hollow of your arm. No, you don't have to grab him with the other hand. Let him kick his legs if he wants to. See, he is looking up at you! Yes, I believe he is. Do you see Daddy? Do you, precious?"

"Must be some sight," I murmurs. "What am I supposed to do now?"

"Oh, you may rock him gently, if you like," says Vee. "And I don't suppose he'd mind if you sang a bit."

"Wouldn't that be takin' a mean advantage?" says I.

Vee laughs and goes off so I can practice alone, which was thoughtful of her.

I didn't find it so bad this time. I discovers I can wiggle my toes occasionally without lettin' him crash on to the floor. And I begun to get used to lookin' at him at close range, too. His nose don't seem quite so hopeless as it did. I shouldn't wonder but what he'd grow a reg'lar nose there in time. And their little ears are cute, ain't they? But say, it was them big blue eyes that got me interested. First off they sort of wandered around the room aimless; but after a while they steadies down into gazin' at me sort of curious and admirin'. I rather liked that.

"How about it, Snookums?" says I. "What do you think of your amateur daddy? Or are you wonderin' if your hair'll be as red as mine? Don't you care. There's worse things in life than bein' bright on top. Eh? Think you'd like to get your fingers in it? Might burny-burn. Well, try it once, if you like." And I ducks my head so he can reach that wavin' forelock of mine.

"Googly-goo!" remarks Sonny, indicatin' 'most anything you're a mind to call it.

Anyway, he seems to be entertained. We was gettin' acquainted fast. Pretty soon he pulls a smile on me. Say, it's the real thing in the smile line, too—confidential and chummy. I has to smile back.

"That's the trick, Buster!" says I. "Friendly face motions is what wins."

"Goo-oogly-goo!" says he.

"True words!" says I. "I believe you."

We must have kept that up for near half an hour, until he shows signs of gettin' sleepy. Just before he drops off, though, he was wavin' one of his hands around, and the first thing I know them soft little pink fingers has circled about my thumb.

Say, that turned the trick—just that. Ever had a baby grip you that way? Your own, I mean? If you have, I expect you'll know what I'm drivin' at. And if you ain't—well, you got something comin' to you. It's a thing I couldn't tell you about. It's a gentle sort of thrill, that spreads and spreads until it gets 'way inside of you—under your vest, on the left side.

When Vee finally comes in to see how we're gettin' along, he's snoozin' calm and peaceful, with a sketchy smile kind of flickerin' on and off that rosebud mouth of his, like he was indulgin' in pleasant dreams. Also, them little pink fingers was still wrapped around my thumb.

"Well, if you aren't a picture, you two!" says Vee, bendin' over and whisperin' in my ear.

"This ain't a pose," says I. "It's the real thing."

"You mean—" begins Vee.

"I mean I've qualified," says I. "Maybe I didn't show up so

strong durin' the initiation, but I squeaked through. I'm a reg'lar daddy now. See! He's givin' me the inside brother grip—on my thumb. You can call Auntie in, if you like."

CHAPTER XVII

A LOW TACKLE BY TORCHY

What I like about livin' out in the forty-minute-if-you're-lucky sector is that, once you get here, it's so nice and quiet. You don't have to worry, when you turn in at night, about manhole covers bein' blown through your front windows, or whether the basement floor will drop into the subway, or if some gun gang is going to use your street for a shootin' gallery. All you do is douse the lights and feel sure nothin's going to happen until breakfast.

We were talkin' something along this line the other evenin', Vee and me, sayin' how restful and soothin' these spring nights in the country was—you know, sort of handin' it to ourselves. And it couldn't have been more'n two hours later that I'm routed rude out of the downy by the 'phone bell. It's buzzin' away frantic. I scrambles out and fits the receiver to my ear just in time to get the full benefit of the last half of a long ring.

"Ah, take your thumb off," I sings out to the night operator. "Who you think you're callin'—the fire house or some doctor?"

"Here's your party," I hears her remark cheerful, and then

this other voice comes in.

Well, it's Norton Plummer, that fussy little lawyer neighbor of ours who lives about half a mile the other side of the railroad. Since he's been made chairman of the local Council of Defense and put me on as head of one of his committees, he's rung me up frequent, generally at dinner-time, to ask if I have anything to report. Seems to think, just because I'm a reserve lieutenant on special detail, that I ought to be discoverin' spies and diggin' out plots every few minutes.

"Yes, yes," says I. "This is me. What then?"

"Did you read about that German naval officer who escaped from an internment camp last week?" he asks.

"But that was 'way down in North Carolina or somewhere, wasn't it?" says I.

"Perhaps," says Plummer. "But he isn't there now. He's here."

"Eh?" says I. "Where?"

"Prowling around my house," says Plummer. "That is, he was a few moments ago. My chauffeur saw him. So did I. He's on his way down towards the trolley line now."

"Why didn't you nab him?" I asks.

"Me?" says Plummer. "Why, he's a huge fellow, and no doubt a desperate man. I presume he was after me: I don't know."

"But how'd you come to spot him as a Hun officer?" says I.

"By the description I read," says he. "It fits perfectly. There's no telling what he's up to around here. And listen: I have telephoned to the Secret Service headquarters in town for them to send some men out in a machine. But they'll be nearly an hour on the road, at best. Meanwhile, what we must do is to prevent him from catching that last trolley car, which goes in about twelve-fifteen. We must stop him, you see."

"Oh, must we?" says I. "Listens to me like some he-sized job."

"That's why I called you up," says Plummer. "You know where the line crosses the railroad? Well, he'll probably try to get on there. Hurry down and prevent him."

"Is that all I have to do?" says I. "What's the scheme—do I trip him up and sit on his head?"

"No, no!" says Plummer. "Don't attempt violence. He's a powerful man. Why, my chauffeur saw him break the chain on our back gate as if it had been nothing but twine. Just gave it a push—and snap it went. Oh, he's strong as a bull. Ill-tempered, too."

"Huh!" says I. "And I'm to go down and—Say, where do you come in on this?"

"I'll be there with John just as soon as we can quiet Mrs. Plummer and the maids," says he. "They're almost in hysterics. In the meantime, though, if you could get there and—Well, use strategy of some kind. Anything to keep him from catching that car. You understand?"

"I get you," says I. "And it don't sound encitin' at all. But I'll see what I can do. If you find me smeared all over the road, though, you'll know I didn't pull it off. Also, I'd suggest that you make that soothin' act of yours speedy."

Course this wakes Vee up, and she wants to know what it's all about.

"Oh, a little private panic that Norton Plummer is indulgin' in," says I. "Nothin' to get fidgety over. I'll be back soon."

"But—but you won't be reckless, will you, Torchy?" she asks.

"Who, me?" says I. "How foolish. Why, I invented that 'Safety First' motto, and side-steppin' trouble is the easiest thing I do. Trust me."

I expect she was some nervous, at that. But she's a good sport, Vee.

"If you're needed," says she, "of course I want you to go. But do be careful."

I didn't need any coaxin'. Somehow, I never could get used to roamin' around in the country after dark. Always seemed sort of spooky. Bein' brought up in the city, I expect, where the scenery is illuminated constant, accounts for that. So, as I slips out the front gate and down towards the station, I keeps in the middle of the road and glances suspicious at the tree shadows.

Not that I was takin' Plummer's Hun scare real serious. He'd had a bad case of spy fever recent. Why, only last week he got all stirred up over what he announced was a private wireless outfit that he'd discovered somewhere in the outskirts of Flushing; and when they came to trail it down it turns out to be some new wire clothes-line strung up back of a flat buildin'.

Besides, what would an escaped German naval officer be doin' up this way? He'd be more apt to strike for Mexico, wouldn't he? Still, long as I'd let Plummer put me on the committee, it was up to me to answer any calls. Might be entertainin' to see who he'd mistaken for an enemy alien this time. And if all I was expected to do was spill a little impromptu strategy—well, maybe I could, and then again maybe I couldn't. I'd take a look, anyway.

It was seein' a light in Danny Shea's little cottage, back on a side lane, that gave me my original hunch. Danny is one of the important officials of the Long Island Railroad, if you let him tell it. He's the flagman down where the highway and trolley line cross the tracks at grade, and when his rheumatism ain't makin' him grouchy he's more or less amusin' to chin with.

Danny had pestered the section boss until he'd got him to build a little square coop for him, there by the crossin'—a place where he could crawl in between trains, smoke his pipe, and toast himself over a sheet-iron stove about as big as a picnic coffee-pot.

And that sentry-box effect was the pride of Danny's heart. Most of his spare time and all the money he could bone out of the commuters he spent in improvin' and decoratin' it. He'd cut a couple of round windows, like port-holes, and fitted 'em with swingin' sashes. Then he'd tacked on some flower-boxes underneath and filled 'em with geraniums.

When he wasn't waterin' his flowers or coaxin' along his little grass-plot or addin' another shelf inside, he was paintin' the outside. Danny's idea of a swell color scheme seemed to be to get on as many different shades as possible. The roof was red, the sides a bright blue. But where he spread himself was on the trim. All you had to do to get on the right side of Danny was to lug him out a half-pound can of paint different from any he'd applied so far. He'd use it somehow.

So the window-sashes was picked out in yellow, the side battens loomed up prominent as black lines, and the door-panels was a pale pink. Nearly all the commuters had been touched by Danny for something or other that could be added to the shack. Only a week or so before, I'd got in strong with him by contributin' a new padlock for the door— a vivid red one, like they have on the village jail in vaudeville plays.

And it struck me now that if I had the key to that little box of Danny's it would make a perfectly good listenin'-post for any midnight sleuthin' I had to do. Most likely he was up dosin' himself or bathin' his joints.

Well, he was. He didn't seem any too enthusiastic about lettin' me have the key, though.

"I dunno," says he. "'Tis railroad property, y' understand, and I'd be afther riskin' me job if any thin' should—"

"I know, Danny," says I. "But you tell 'em it was commandeered by the U. S. Army, which is me; and if that don't square you I'll have Mr. Baker come on and tell the section boss where he gets off."

"Verra well," says Danny. And in less than five minutes more I'm down there at the crossin', all snug and cozy, peekin' out of them round windows into No Man's Land.

For a while it was kind of excitin'; but after that it got sort of monotonous. There was about half of an old moon in the sky, and only a few clouds, so you could see fairly well—if there'd been anything to see. But nothing seemed to be stirrin', up or down the road.

What a nut that Norton Plummer was, anyway, feedin' me up with his wild tales in the middle of the night! And why didn't he show up? Finally I got restless, and walked out where I could rubber up the trolley track. No sign or sound of a car. Then I looks at my watch again, and figures out it ain't due for twenty minutes or so. Next I strolls across the railroad to look for Plummer. And, just as I'm passin' a big maple tree, out steps this huge party with the whiskers. I nearly jumped out of my puttees.

"Eh?" says I gaspy.

"Gotta match?" says he.

"I—I guess so," says I.

I reached as far as I could when I hands him the box, too. He's a whale of a man, tall and bulky. And his whiskers are the bristly kind—straw-colored, I should say. He's wearin' a double-breasted blue coat and a sort of yachtin' cap. Uh-huh! Plummer must have been right. If this gink wasn't a Hun naval officer, then what was he? The ayes had it.

He produces a pipe and starts to light up. One match broke, the second had no strikin' head on it, the third just fizzed.

"Gr-r-r-r!" says he.

Then he starts for the crossin', me trailin' along. I saw he had his eye on Danny's sentry-box, meanin' to get in the lee of it. Even then I didn't have any bright little idea.

Sewell Ford

"Waitin' for the trolley?" I throws out.

"What of it?" he growls.

"Oh, no offense," says I hasty. "Maybe there are others."

He just lets out another grunt, and tries one more match with his face up against the side of the shanty. And then, all in a jump, my bean got into gear.

"You might have better luck inside," says I, swingin' open the door invitin'.

He don't even say thank you. He ain't one of that kind. For a second or so I thought he wasn't goin' to take any notice; but after one more failure he steps around, inspects the inside of the shanty, and then squeezes himself through the door. At that, he wasn't all the way in, but by the time he had a match goin' I'd got my nerve back.

"Ah, take the limit, Cap'n," says I.

With that I plants one foot impulsive right where he was widest, gives a quick shove, slams the door shut behind him, and snaps the big padlock through the hasp.

"Hey!" he sings out startled. "What the—"

"Now, don't get messy, Cap'n," says I. "You're in, ain't you? Smoke up and be happy."

"You—you loafer!" he gurgles throaty. "What do you mean?"

"Just a playful little prank, Cap," says I. "Don't get excited. You're perfectly safe."

Maybe he was. But some folks don't appreciate little attentions like that. The Cap'n starts in bumpin' and thrashin' violent in there, like a pup that's crawled into a drainpipe and got himself stuck. He hammers on the walls with his fists, throws his weight against the door, and tries to kick his way out.

But the section boss must have used rail spikes and reinforced the studdin' with fishplates when he built that coop for Danny, or else the big Hun was too tight a fit to get full play for his strength. Anyway, all he did was make the little house rock until you'd thought Long Island was enjoyin' a young earthquake. Meanwhile I stands by, ready to do a sprint if he should break loose, and offers more or less cheerin' advice.

"Easy with your elbows in there, Cap," says I. "You're assaultin' railroad property, you know, and if you do any damage you can be pinched for malicious mischief."

"You—you better let me out of here quick!" he roars. "I gotta get back."

"Oh, you'll get to town all right," says I. "I'll promise you that."

"Loafer!" he snorts.

"Say, how do you know I ain't sensitive on that point?" says I. "You might hurt my feelin's."

"Gr-r-r!" says he. "I would wring your neck."

"Such a disposition!" says I.

Oh, yes, we swapped quite a little repartee, me and the

Cap'n, or whatever he was. But, instead of his bein' soothed by it he gets more strenuous every minute. He had that shack rockin' like a boat.

Next thing I saw was one of his big feet stickin' out under the bottom sill. Then I remembers that the sentry-box has only a dirt floor—on account of the stove, I expect. Course Danny has banked the outside up with sod for five or six inches, but that ain't enough to hold it down with a human tornado cuttin' loose inside. A minute more and another foot appears on the other side, and the next I knew the whole shootin' match begins to rise, wabbly but sure, until he's lifted it almost to his knees.

Looked like the Cap'n was goin' to shed the coop over his head, as you'd shuck a shirt, and I was edgin' away prepared to make a run for it. But right there the elevatin' process stops, and after some violent squirms there comes an outburst of language that would only get the delete sign if I should give it. I could dope out what had happened. That plank seat across one side had caught the Cap'n about where he buckles his belt, and he couldn't budge it any further.

"Want a shoe-horn, Cap'n?" I asks. "Say, next time you try wearin' a kiosk as a slip-on sweater you'd better train down for the act."

"Gr-r-r-r!" says he. "I—I will teach you to play your jokes on me, young whipper-snap."

He does some more writhin', and pretty soon manages to swing open one of the port-holes. With his face up to that, like a deep-sea diver peekin' out o' his copper bonnet, he starts for me, kickin' over the little stove as he gets under way, and tearin' the whole thing loose from the foundation.

Course he's some handicapped by the hobble-skirt effect around his knees, and the weight above his shoulders makes him a bit topheavy; but, at that, he can get over the ground as fast as I can walk backwards.

Must have been kind of a weird sight, there in the moonlight—me bein' pursued up the road by this shack with legs under it, the little tin smoke-pipe wavin' jaunty about nine feet in the air, and the geraniums in the flower-boxes noddin' jerky.

"Say, what do you think you are?" I calls out. "A wooden tank goin' over the top?"

I was sort of wonderin' how long he could keep this up, and what would be the finish, when from behind me I hears this spluttery line of exclamations indicatin' rage. It's Danny, who's got anxious about lettin' me have the use of his coop and has come down to see what's happenin' to it. Well, he saw.

"Hey! Stop him, stop him!" he yells.

"Stop him yourself, Danny," says I.

"But he's runnin' away with me little flag-house, thief of the worruld!" howls Danny. "It's breakin' and enterin' and carryin' away th' property of the Long Island Railroad that he's guilty of."

"Yes; I've explained all that to him," says I.

"Go back and come'out of that, ye thievin' Dutchman!" orders Danny, rushin' up and bangin' on the door with his fists.

"Just let me out, you Irish shrimp!" snarls the Cap'n.

"Can't be done—not yet, Danny," says I.

"But—but he's destroyin' me flowers and runnin' off with me little house," protested Danny. "I'll have the law on him, so I will."

"Get out, Irisher, or I'll fall on you," warns the Cap'n.

And right in the midst of this debate I sees Norton Plummer and his chauffeur hurryin' up from across the tracks. I skips back to meet 'em.

"Well," says Plummer, "have you seen anything of the escaped prisoner?"

"That's him," says I, pointin' to the wabblin' shack.

"Whaddye mean?" says Plummer, starin' puzzled.

"He's inside," says I. "You said use strategy, didn't you? Well, that's the best I had in stock. I got him boxed, all right, but he won't stay put. He insists on playin' the human turtle. What'll we do with him now? Come see."

"My word!" says Plummer, as he gets a view of the Cap'n's legs and the big whiskered face at the little window. "So there you are, eh, you runaway Hun?"

"Bah!" says the Cap'n. "Why do you call me Hun?"

"Because I've identified you as an escaped German naval officer," says Plummer. "Do you deny it?"

"Me?" says the Cap'n. "Bah!"

"Who do you claim to be, then?" says I. "A tourist Eskimo or an out-of-town buyer from Patagonia?"

"I'm Nels Petersen, that's who I am," says he, "and I'm chief engineer of a ferry-boat that's due to make her first run at five-thirty-three."

"What!" says Plummer. "Are you the Swede engineer who has been writing love letters to—Say, what is the name of Mrs. Plummer's maid?"

"Selma," says the Cap'n.

"By George!" says Plummer. "I believe the man's right. But see here: what were you doing prowling around my back yard to-night! Why didn't you go to the servants' entrance and ask the cook for Selma, if you're as much in love with her as you've written that you are?"

"What do you know about it?" demands Petersen.

"Good Lord!" gasps Plummer. "Haven't I had to puzzle out all those wretched scrawls of yours and read 'em to her? Such mushy letters, too! Come, if you're the man, why didn't you call Selma out and tell her all that to her face?"

Nothing but heavy breathing from inside the shack.

"You don't mean to say you were too bashful!" goes on Plummer. "A great big fellow like you!"

If it hadn't been for the whiskers I believe we could have seen him blush.

"Look here," says Plummer. "You may be what you say you are, and then again you may not. Perhaps you just guessed at the girl's name. We can't afford to take any chances. The only way to settle it is to send for Selma."

"No, no!" pleads the big gink. "Please! Not like this."

"Yes, just like that," insists Plummer. "Only, if you'd rather, you can carry your house back where it belongs and sit down. John, run home and bring Selma here."

Well, we had our man nicely tamed now. With Selma liable to show up, he was ready to do as he was told. Just why, we couldn't make out. Anyway, he hobbles back to the crossin' and eases the shack down where he found it. Also, he slumps inside on the bench and waits, durin' which proceedin' the last trolley goes boomin' past.

Inside of ten minutes John is back with the maid. Kind of a slim, classy-lookin' girl she is, too. And when Selma sees that big face at the round window there's no doubt about his being the chosen one.

"Oh, Nels, Nels!" she wails out. "Vy you don'd coom by the house yet?"

"I was scart, Selma," says Nels, "for fear you'd tell me to go away."

"But—but I don'd, Nels," says Selma.

"Shall I let him out for the fade-away scene?" says I.

Plummer nods. And we had to turn our backs as they go to the fond clinch.

Accordin' to Plummer, Selma had been waitin' for Nels to say the word for more'n a year, and for the last two months she'd been so absent-minded and moody that she hadn't been of much use around the house. But him gettin' himself boxed up as an escaped Hun had sort of broken the ice.

"There, now!" says Plummer. "You two go back to the house and talk it over. You may have until three-fifteen to settle all details, and then I'll have John drive Petersen down to his ferry-boat. Be sure and fix the day, though. I don't want to go through another night like this."

"But what about me little lawn," demands Danny, "that's tore up entirely? And who's to mend me stove-pipe and all?"

"Oh, here's something that will cover all that, Danny," says Plummer, slippin' him a ten-spot. "And I've no doubt Petersen will contribute something, too."

"Sure!" says Nels, fishin' in his pockets.

"Two bits!" says Danny, pickin' up the quarter scornful. "Thim Swedes are the tightwads! And if ever I find this wan kidnappin' me little house again—"

At which Danny breaks off and shakes his fist menacin'.

When I gets back home I tiptoes upstairs; but Vee is only dozin', and wakes up with a jump.

"Is that you, Torchy?" says she. "Has—has anything dreadful happened?"

"Yes," says I. "I had to pull a low tackle, and Danny Shea's declared war on Sweden."

CHAPTER XVIII

TAG DAY AT TORCHY'S

Course, in a way, it was our fault, I expect. We never should have let on that there was any hitch about what we was goin' to name the baby. Blessed if I know now just how it got around. I remember Vee and I havin' one or two little talks on the subject, but I don't think we'd tackled the proposition real serious.

You see, at first we were too busy sort of gettin' used to havin' him around and framin' up a line on this parent act we was supposed to put over. Anyway, I was. And for three or four weeks, there, I called him anything that came handy, from Young Sport to Old Snoodlekins. Vee she sticks to Baby. Uh-huh—just plain Baby. But the way she says it, breathin' it out kind of soft and gentle, sounded perfectly all right to me.

And the youngster didn't seem to have any kick comin'. He was gettin' so he'd look up and coo real intelligent when she speaks to him in that fashion. You couldn't blame him, for it was easy to listen to.

As for the different things I called him—well, he didn't mind them, either. No matter what it was,—Old Pink Toes or

Wiggle-heels,—he'd generally pass it off with a smile, providin' he wasn't too busy with his bottle or tryin' to get hold of his foot with both of his hands.

Then one day Auntie, who's been listenin' disapprovin' all the while, just can't hold in any longer.

"Isn't it high time," says she, "that you addressed the child properly by his right name?"

"Eh?" says I, gawpin'. "Which one?"

"You don't mean to say," she goes on, "that you have not yet decided on his baptismal name?"

"I didn't know he was a Baptist," says I feeble.

"We hadn't quite settled what to call him," says Vee.

"Besides," I adds, "I don't see the use bein' in a rush about it. Maybe were're savin' that up."

"Saving!" says Auntie. "For what reason?"

"Oh, general conservation," says I. "Got the habit. We've had heatless Mondays and wheatless Wednesdays and fryless Fridays and sunless Sundays, so why not nameless babies?"

Auntie sniffs and goes off with her nose in the air, as she always does whenever I spring any of my punk persiflage on her.

But then Vee takes it up, and says Auntie is right and that we really ought to decide on a name and begin using it.

"Oh, very well," says I. "I'll be thinking one up."

Seemed simple enough. Course, I'd never named any babies before, but I had an idea I could dig out half a dozen good, serviceable monickers between then and dinner-time.

Somehow, though, I couldn't seem to hit on anything that I was willing to wish on to the youngster offhand. When I got right up against the problem, it seemed kind of serious.

Why, here was something he'd have to live with all his life; us, too. We'd have to say it over maybe a hundred times a day. And if he grew up and amounted to anything, as we was sure he would, it would mean that this front name of his that I had to pick out might be displayed more or less prominent. It would be on his office door, on his letterheads, on his cards. He'd sign it to checks.

Maybe it would be printed in the newspapers, used in headlines, or painted on campaign banners. Might be displayed on billboards. Who could tell?

And the deeper I got into the thing the more I wabbled about from one name to another, until I wondered how people had the nerve to give their children some of the tags you hear— Percy, Isadore, Lulu, Reginald, and so on. And do it so casual, too. Why, I knew of a couple who named their three girls after parlor-cars; and a gink in Brooklyn who called one of his boys Prospect, after the park. Think of loadin' a helpless youngster with anything freaky like that!

Besides, how were you going to know that even the best name you could pick wouldn't turn out to be a misfit? About the only Percy I ever knew in real life was a great two-fisted husk who was foreman of a stereotypin' room; and here in the Corrugated Buildin', if you'll come in some night after five, I can show you a wide built scrub lady, with hair redder'n mine and a voice like a huckster—her front name is

Violet. Yet I expect, when them two was babies, both those names sounded kind of cute. I could see where it would be easy enough for me to make a mistake that it would take a court order to straighten out.

So, when Vee asks if I've made any choice yet I had to admit that I'm worse muddled up on the subject than when I started in. All I can do is hand over a list I've copied down on the back of an envelop with every one of 'em checked off as no good.

"Let's see," says Vee, glancin' 'em over curious. "Lester. Why, I'm sure that is rather a nice name for a boy."

"Yes," says I; "but after I put it down I remembered a Lester I knew once. He was a simp that wore pink neckties and used to write love-letters to Mary Pickford."

"What about Earl?" she asks.

"Too flossy," says I. "Sounds like you was tryin' to let on he belonged to the aristocracy."

"Well, Donald, then," says she. "That's a good, sensible name."

"But we ain't Scotch," I objects.

"What's the matter with Philip?" says Vee.

"I can never remember whether it has one *l* and two *p*'s or the other way round."

"But you haven't considered any of the common ones," goes on Vee, "such as John or William or Thomas or James or Arthur."

"Because that would mean he'd be called Bill or Tom or Art," says I. "Besides, I kind of thought he ought to have something out of the usual run—one you wouldn't forget as soon as you heard it."

"If I may suggest," breaks in Auntie, "the custom of giving the eldest son the family name of his mother is rather a good one. Had you considered Hemmingway?"

I just gasps and glances at Vee. What if she should fall for anything like that! Think of smotherin' a baby under most of the alphabet all at one swoop! And imagine a boy strugglin' through schooldays and vacations with all that tied to him.

Hemmingway! Why, he'd grow up round-shouldered and knock-kneed, and most likely turn out to be a floor-walker in the white goods department, or the manager of a gift-shop tearoom. Hemmingway!

Just the thought of it made me dizzy; and I begun breathin' easier when I saw Vee shake her head.

"He's such a little fellow, Auntie," says she. "Wouldn't that be—well, rather topheavy?"

Which disposes of Auntie. She admits maybe it would. But from then on, as the news seems to spread that we was havin' a kind of deadlock with the namin' process, the volunteers got busy. Old Leon Battou, our butler-cook, hinted that his choice would be Emil.

"For six generations," says he, "Emil has been the name of the first-born son in our family."

"That's stickin' to tradition," says I. "It sounds perfectly swell, too, when you know how to pronounce it. But, you see, we're foundin' a new dynasty."

Mr. Robert don't say so outright, but he suggests that Ellins Ballard wouldn't be such a bad combination.

"True," he adds, "the governor and I deserve no such distinction; but I'm sure we would both be immensely flattered. And there's no telling how reckless we might be when it come to presenting christening cups and that sort of thing."

"That's worth rememberin'," says I. "And I expect you wouldn't mind, in case you had a boy to name later on, callin' him Torchy, eh!"

Mr. Robert grins. "Entry withdrawn," says he.

How this Amelia Gaston Leroy got the call to crash in on our little family affair, though, I couldn't quite dope out. We never suspected before that she was such an intimate friend of ours. Course, since we'd been livin' out in the Piping Rock section we had seen more or less of her—more, as a rule. She was built that way.

Oh, yes. Amelia was one of the kind that could bounce in among three or four people in a thirty by forty-five living-room and make the place seem crowded. Mr. Robert's favorite description of her was that one half of Amelia didn't know how the other half lived. To state it plain, Amelia was some whale of a girl. One look at her, and you did no more guessin' as to what caused the food shortage.

I got the shock of my life, too, when they told me she was the one that wrote so much of this mushy magazine poetry you see printed. For all the lady poetesses I'd ever seen had been thin, shingled-chested parties with mud-colored hair and soulful eyes.

There was nothing thin about Amelia. Her eyes might have been soulful enough at times, but mostly I'd seen 'em fixed on a tray of sandwiches or a plate of layer cake.

They'd had her up at the Ellinses' once or twice when they were givin' one of their musical evenin's, and she'd spouted some of her stuff.

Her first call on us, though, was when she blew in last Sunday afternoon and announced that she'd come to see "that dear, darling man child" of ours. And for a girl of her size Amelia is some breeze, take it from me. Honest, for the first ten minutes or so there I felt like our happy little home had been hit by a young tornado.

"Where is he?" she demands. "Please take me at once into the regal presence of his youthful majesty."

I noticed Vee sizin' her up panicky, and I knew she was thinkin' of what might happen to them spindle-legged white chairs in the nursery.

"How nice of you to want to see him!" says Vee. "But let me have Baby brought down here. Just a moment."

And she steers her towards a solid built davenport that we'd been meanin' to have reupholstered anyway. Then we was treated to a line of high-brow gush as Amelia inspects the youngster through her shell lorgnette and tries to tell us in impromptu blank verse how wonderful he is.

"Ah, he is one of the sun children, loved of the high gods," says she, rollin' her eyes. "He comes to you wearing the tints of dawn and trailing clouds of glory. You remember how

Wordsworth puts it?"

As she fires this straight at me, I has to say something.

"Does he?" I asks.

"I am always impressed," she gurgles on, "by the calm serenity in the eyes of these little ones. It is as if they—"

But just then Snoodlekins begins screwin' up his face. He's never been mauled around by a lady poetess before, or maybe it was just because there was so much of her. Anyway, he tears loose with a fine large howl and the serenity stuff is all off. It takes Vee four or five minutes to soothe him.

Meanwhile Miss Leroy gets around to statin' the real reason why we're bein' honored.

"I understand," says she, "that you have not as yet chosen a name for him. So I am going to help you. I adore it. I have always wanted to name a baby, and I've never been allowed. Think of that! My brother has five children, too; but he would not listen to any of my suggestions.

"So I am aunt to a Walter who should have been called Clifford, and a Margaret whom I wanted to name Beryl, and so on. Even my laundress preferred to select names for her twins from some she had seen on a circus poster rather than let me do it for her.

"But I am sure you are rational young people, and recognize that I have some natural talent in that direction. Names! Why, I have made a study of them. I must, you see, in my writing. And this dear little fellow deserves something fitting. Now let me see. Ah, I have it! He shall be Cedric—

after Cedric the Red, you know."

Accordin' to her, it was all settled. She heaves herself up off the davenport, straightens her hat, and prepares to leave, smilin' satisfied, like an expert who's been called in and has finished the job.

"We—we will consider Cedric," says Vee. "Thank you so much."

"Oh, not at all," says Amelia. "Of course, if I should happen to think of anything better within the next few days I will let you know at once." And out she floats.

Vee gazes after her and sighs.

"I suppose Cedric is rather a good name," says she, "but somehow I don't feel like using one that a stranger has picked out for us. Do you, Torchy?"

"You've said it," says I. "I'd sooner let her buy my neckties, or tell me how I should have my eggs cooked for breakfast."

"And yet," says Vee, "unless we can think of something better—"

"We will," says I. "I'm goin' through them pages in the back of the big dictionary."

In less'n half an hour there's a knock at the door, and here's a chauffeur come with a note from Amelia. On the way home she's had another hunch.

"After all," she writes, "Cedric seems rather too harsh, too rough-shod. So I have decided on Lucian."

"Huh!" says I. "She's decided, has she? Say, whose tag day is this, anyway—ours or hers?"

Vee shrugs her shoulders.

"I'm not sure that we should like calling him Lucian; it's so—so—"

"I know," says I, "so perfectly sweet. Say, can't we block Amelia off somehow? Suppose I send back word that a rich step-uncle has promised to leave him a ton of coal if we call the baby Ebenezer after him?"

Vee chuckles.

"Oh, no doubt she'll forget all about it by morning," says she.

Seems we'd just begun hearin' from the outside districts, though, or else they'd been savin' up their ideas for this particular afternoon and evenin'; for between then and nine o'clock no less'n half a dozen different parties dropped in, every last one of 'em with a name to register. And their contributions ranged all the way from Aaron to Xury. There were two rooters for Woodrow and one for Pershing.

Some of the neighbors were real serious about it. They told us what a time they'd had namin' some of their children, brought up cases where families had been busted up over such discussions, and showed us where their choice couldn't be beat. One merry bunch from the Country Club thought they was pullin' something mighty humorous when they stopped in to tell us how they'd held a votin' contest on the subject, and that the winnin' combination was, Paul Roger.

"After something you read on a cork, eh?" says I. "Much obliged. And I hope nobody strained his intellect."

"The idea!" says Vee, after they've rolled off. "Voting on such a thing at a club! Just as if Baby was a battleship, or a— a new moving-picture place. I think that's perfectly horrid of them."

"It was fresh, all right," says I. "But I expect we got to stand for such guff until we can give out that we've found a name that suits us. Lemme tackle that list again. Now, how would Russell do? Russell Ballard? No; too many *l*'s and *r*'s. Here's Chester. And I expect the boys would call him Chesty. Then there's Clyde. But there's steamship line by that name. What about Stanley? Oh, yes; he was an explorer."

I admit I was gettin' desperate about then. I was flounderin' around in a whole ocean of names, long ones and short ones, fancy and plain, yet I couldn't quite make up my mind. I'd mussed my hair, shed my collar, and scribbled over sheets and sheets of paper, without gettin' anywhere at all. And when I gave up and turned in about eleven-thirty, my head was so muddled I wouldn't have had the nerve to have named a pet kitten.

I must have just dozed off to sleep when I hears this bell ringin' somewhere. I couldn't quite make out whether it was a fire alarm, or the *z*'s in the back of the dictionary goin' off, when Vee calls out that it's the 'phone.

I tumbles out and paws around for the extension.

"Wha-what?" says I. "What the blazes! Ye-uh. This is me. Wha-wha's matter?"

And then comes this gurgly voice at the other end of the wire. It's our old friend Amelia.

"Do you know," says she, "I have just thought of the

loveliest name for your dear baby."

"Oh, have you?" says I, sort of crisp.

"Yes," says she, "and I simply couldn't wait until morning to tell you. Now listen—it's Ethelbert."

"Ethel-Bert!" says I, gaspy. "Say, you know he's no mixed foursome."

"No, no," says she. Ethelbert—one name, after the old Saxon king. Ethelbert Ballard. "Isn't that just perfect? And I am so glad it came to me."

I couldn't agree with her real enthusiastic, so it's lucky she hung up just as she did.

"Huh!" I remarks to Vee. "Why not Maryjim or Daisybill? Say, I think our friend Amelia must have gone off her hinge."

But Vee only yawns and advises me to go to sleep and forget it. Well, I tried. You know how it is, though, when you've been jolted out of the feathers just as you're halfway through the first reel of the slumber stuff. I couldn't get back, to save me.

I counted sheep jumpin' over a wall, I tried lookin' down a railroad track until I could seen the rails meet, and I spelled Constantinople backwards. Nothing doing in the Morpheus act.

I was wider awake then than a new taxi driver makin' his first trip up Broadway. I could think of swell names for seashore cottages, for new surburban additions, and for other people's babies. I invented an explosive pretzel that would

Sewell Ford

win the war. I thought of bills I ought to pay next week sure, and of what I meant to tell the laundryman if he kept on making hash of my pet shirts.

Then I got to wonderin' about this old-maid poetess. Was she through for the night, or did she work double shifts? If she wasn't any nearer sleep than I was she might think up half a dozen substitutes for Ethelbert before mornin'. Would she insist on springin' each one on me as they hit her?

Maybe she was gettin' ready to call me again now. Should I pretend not to hear and let her ring, or would it be better to answer and let on that this was Police Headquarters?

Honest, I got so fidgety waitin' for that buzzer to go off that I could almost hear the night operator pluggin' in on our wire.

And then a thought struck me that wouldn't let go. So, slippin' out easy and throwin' on a bath-robe, I sneaked downstairs to the back hall 'phone, turned on the light, and hunted up Miss Leroy's number in the book.

"Give her a good strong ring, please," says I to Exchange, "and keep it up until you rouse somebody."

"Leave it to me," says the operator. And in a minute or so I gets this throaty "Hello!"

"Miss Leroy?" says I.

"Yes," says she. "Who is calling?"

"Ballard," says I. "I'm the fond parent of the nameless baby. And say, do you still stick to Ethelbert?"

"Why," says she, "I—er—"

"I just wanted to tell you," I goes on, "that this guessin' contest closes at 3 A.M., and if you want to make any more entries you got only forty minutes to get 'em in. Nighty-night."

And I rings off just as she begins sputterin' indignant.

That seems to help a lot, and inside of five minutes I'm snoozin' peaceful.

It was next mornin' at breakfast that Vee observes offhand, as though the subject hadn't been mentioned before:

"About naming the baby, now."

"Ye-e-es?" says I, smotherin' a groan.

"Why couldn't we call him after you?" she asks.

"Not—not Richard Junior?" says I.

"Well, after both of us, then," says she. "Richard Hemmingway. It—it is what I've wanted to name him all along."

"You have?" says I. "Well, for the love of—"

"You didn't ask me, that's why," says she.

"Why—why, so I didn't," says I. "And say, Vee, I don't know who's got a better right. As for my part of the name, I've used it so little it's almost as good as new. Richard Hemmingway Ballard it shall be."

"Oh, I'm so glad," says she. "Of course, I did want you to be the one to pick it out; but if you're satisfied with—"

"Satisfied!" says I. "Why, I'm tickled to pieces. And here you had that up your sleeve all the while!"

Vee smiles and nods.

"We must have the christening very soon," says she, "so everyone will know."

"You bet!" says I. "And I've a good notion to put it on the train bulletin down at the station, too. First off, though, we'd better tell young Richard himself and see how he likes it. I expect, though, unless his next crop of hair comes out a different tint from this one, that he'll have to answer to 'Young Torchy' for a good many years."

"Oh, yes," says Vee; "but I'm sure he won't mind that in the least."

"Good girl!" says I, movin' round where I can express my feelin's better.

"Don't!" says Vee. "You'll spill the coffee."

Choose from Thousands of 1stWorldLibrary Classics By

A. M. Barnard
Ada Leverson
Adolphus William Ward
Aesop
Agatha Christie
Alexander Aaronsohn
Alexander Kielland
Alexandre Dumas
Alfred Gatty
Alfred Ollivant
Alice Duer Miller
Alice Turner Curtis
Alice Dunbar
Allen Chapman
Alleyne Ireland
Ambrose Bierce
Amelia E. Barr
Amory H. Bradford
Andrew Lang
Andrew McFarland Davis
Andy Adams
Angela Brazil
Anna Alice Chapin
Anna Sewell
Annie Besant
Annie Hamilton Donnell
Annie Payson Call
Annie Roe Carr
Annonaymous
Anton Chekhov
Archibald Lee Fletcher
Arnold Bennett
Arthur C. Benson
Arthur Conan Doyle
Arthur M. Winfield
Arthur Ransome
Arthur Schnitzler
Arthur Train
Atticus
B.H. Baden-Powell
B. M. Bower
B. C. Chatterjee
Baroness Emmuska Orczy
Baroness Orczy
Basil King
Bayard Taylor
Ben Macomber
Bertha Muzzy Bower
Bjornstjerne Bjornson

Booth Tarkington
Boyd Cable
Bram Stoker
C. Collodi
C. E. Orr
C. M. Ingleby
Carolyn Wells
Catherine Parr Traill
Charles A. Eastman
Charles Amory Beach
Charles Dickens
Charles Dudley Warner
Charles Farrar Browne
Charles Ives
Charles Kingsley
Charles Klein
Charles Hanson Towne
Charles Lathrop Pack
Charles Romyn Dake
Charles Whibley
Charles Willing Beale
Charlotte M. Braeme
Charlotte M. Yonge
Charlotte Perkins Stetson
Clair W. Hayes
Clarence Day Jr.
Clarence E. Mulford
Clemence Housman
Confucius
Coningsby Dawson
Cornelis DeWitt Wilcox
Cyril Burleigh
D. H. Lawrence
Daniel Defoe
David Garnett
Dinah Craik
Don Carlos Janes
Donald Keyhoe
Dorothy Kilner
Dougan Clark
Douglas Fairbanks
E. Nesbit
E. P. Roe
E. Phillips Oppenheim
E. S. Brooks
Earl Barnes
Edgar Rice Burroughs
Edith Van Dyne
Edith Wharton

Edward Everett Hale
Edward J. O'Biren
Edward S. Ellis
Edwin L. Arnold
Eleanor Atkins
Eleanor Hallowell Abbott
Eliot Gregory
Elizabeth Gaskell
Elizabeth McCracken
Elizabeth Von Arnim
Ellem Key
Emerson Hough
Emilie F. Carlen
Emily Bronte
Emily Dickinson
Enid Bagnold
Enilor Macartney Lane
Erasmus W. Jones
Ernie Howard Pie
Ethel May Dell
Ethel Turner
Ethel Watts Mumford
Eugene Sue
Eugenie Foa
Eugene Wood
Eustace Hale Ball
Evelyn Everett-green
Everard Cotes
F. H. Cheley
F. J. Cross
F. Marion Crawford
Fannie E. Newberry
Federick Austin Ogg
Ferdinand Ossendowski
Fergus Hume
Florence A. Kilpatrick
Fremont B. Deering
Francis Bacon
Francis Darwin
Frances Hodgson Burnett
Frances Parkinson Keyes
Frank Gee Patchin
Frank Harris
Frank Jewett Mather
Frank L. Packard
Frank V. Webster
Frederic Stewart Isham
Frederick Trevor Hill
Frederick Winslow Taylor

Friedrich Kerst
Friedrich Nietzsche
Fyodor Dostoyevsky
G.A. Henty
G.K. Chesterton
Gabrielle E. Jackson
Garrett P. Serviss
Gaston Leroux
George A. Warren
George Ade
Geroge Bernard Shaw
George Cary Eggleston
George Durston
George Ebers
George Eliot
George Gissing
George MacDonald
George Meredith
George Orwell
George Sylvester Viereck
George Tucker
George W. Cable
George Wharton James
Gertrude Atherton
Gordon Casserly
Grace E. King
Grace Gallatin
Grace Greenwood
Grant Allen
Guillermo A. Sherwell
Gulielma Zollinger
Gustav Flaubert
H. A. Cody
H. B. Irving
H.C. Bailey
H. G. Wells
H. H. Munro
H. Irving Hancock
H. R. Naylor
H. Rider Haggard
H. W. C. Davis
Haldeman Julius
Hall Caine
Hamilton Wright Mabie
Hans Christian Andersen
Harold Avery
Harold McGrath
Harriet Beecher Stowe
Harry Castlemon
Harry Coghill
Harry Houidini

Hayden Carruth
Helent Hunt Jackson
Helen Nicolay
Hendrik Conscience
Hendy David Thoreau
Henri Barbusse
Henrik Ibsen
Henry Adams
Henry Ford
Henry Frost
Henry James
Henry Jones Ford
Henry Seton Merriman
Henry W Longfellow
Herbert A. Giles
Herbert Carter
Herbert N. Casson
Herman Hesse
Hildegard G. Frey
Homer
Honore De Balzac
Horace B. Day
Horace Walpole
Horatio Alger Jr.
Howard Pyle
Howard R. Garis
Hugh Lofting
Hugh Walpole
Humphry Ward
Ian Maclaren
Inez Haynes Gillmore
Irving Bacheller
Isabel Cecilia Williams
Isabel Hornibrook
Israel Abrahams
Ivan Turgenev
J.G.Austin
J. Henri Fabre
J. M. Barrie
J. M. Walsh
J. Macdonald Oxley
J. R. Miller
J. S. Fletcher
J. S. Knowles
J. Storer Clouston
J. W. Duffield
Jack London
Jacob Abbott
James Allen
James Andrews
James Baldwin

James Branch Cabell
James DeMille
James Joyce
James Lane Allen
James Lane Allen
James Oliver Curwood
James Oppenheim
James Otis
James R. Driscoll
Jane Abbott
Jane Austen
Jane L. Stewart
Janet Aldridge
Jens Peter Jacobsen
Jerome K. Jerome
Jessie Graham Flower
John Buchan
John Burroughs
John Cournos
John F. Kennedy
John Gay
John Glasworthy
John Habberton
John Joy Bell
John Kendrick Bangs
John Milton
John Philip Sousa
John Taintor Foote
Jonas Lauritz Idemil Lie
Jonathan Swift
Joseph A. Altsheler
Joseph Carey
Joseph Conrad
Joseph E. Badger Jr
Joseph Hergesheimer
Joseph Jacobs
Jules Vernes
Julian Hawthrone
Julie A Lippmann
Justin Huntly McCarthy
Kakuzo Okakura
Karle Wilson Baker
Kate Chopin
Kenneth Grahame
Kenneth McGaffey
Kate Langley Bosher
Kate Langley Bosher
Katherine Cecil Thurston
Katherine Stokes
L. A. Abbot
L. T. Meade

L. Frank Baum	Owen Johnson	Stephen Crane
Latta Griswold	P.G. Wodehouse	Stewart Edward White
Laura Dent Crane	Paul and Mabel Thorne	Stijn Streuvels
Laura Lee Hope	Paul G. Tomlinson	Swami Abhedananda
Laurence Housman	Paul Severing	Swami Parmananda
Lawrence Beasley	Percy Brebner	T. S. Ackland
Leo Tolstoy	Percy Keese Fitzhugh	T. S. Arthur
Leonid Andreyev	Peter B. Kyne	The Princess Der Ling
Lewis Carroll	Plato	Thomas A. Janvier
Lewis Sperry Chafer	Quincy Allen	Thomas A Kempis
Lilian Bell	R. Derby Holmes	Thomas Anderton
Lloyd Osbourne	R. L. Stevenson	Thomas Bailey Aldrich
Louis Hughes	R. S. Ball	Thomas Bulfinch
Louis Joseph Vance	Rabindranath Tagore	Thomas De Quincey
Louis Tracy	Rahul Alvares	Thomas Dixon
Louisa May Alcott	Ralph Bonehill	Thomas H. Huxley
Lucy Fitch Perkins	Ralph Henry Barbour	Thomas Hardy
Lucy Maud Montgomery	Ralph Victor	Thomas More
Luther Benson	Ralph Waldo Emmerson	Thornton W. Burgess
Lydia Miller Middleton	Rene Descartes	U. S. Grant
Lyndon Orr	Ray Cummings	Upton Sinclair
M. Corvus	Rex Beach	Valentine Williams
M. H. Adams	Rex E. Beach	Various Authors
Margaret E. Sangster	Richard Harding Davis	Vaughan Kester
Margret Howth	Richard Jefferies	Victor Appleton
Margaret Vandercook	Richard Le Gallienne	Victor G. Durham
Margaret W. Hungerford	Robert Barr	Victoria Cross
Margret Penrose	Robert Frost	Virginia Woolf
Maria Edgeworth	Robert Gordon Anderson	Wadsworth Camp
Maria Thompson Daviess	Robert L. Drake	Walter Camp
Mariano Azuela	Robert Lansing	Walter Scott
Marion Polk Angellotti	Robert Lynd	Washington Irving
Mark Overton	Robert Michael Ballantyne	Wilbur Lawton
Mark Twain	Robert W. Chambers	Wilkie Collins
Mary Austin	Rosa Nouchette Carey	Willa Cather
Mary Catherine Crowley	Rudyard Kipling	Willard F. Baker
Mary Cole	Saint Augustine	William Dean Howells
Mary Hastings Bradley	Samuel B. Allison	William le Queux
Mary Roberts Rinehart	Samuel Hopkins Adams	W. Makepeace Thackeray
Mary Rowlandson	Sarah Bernhardt	William W. Walter
M. Wollstonecraft Shelley	Sarah C. Hallowell	William Shakespeare
Maud Lindsay	Selma Lagerlof	Winston Churchill
Max Beerbohm	Sherwood Anderson	Yei Theodora Ozaki
Myra Kelly	Sigmund Freud	Yogi Ramacharaka
Nathaniel Hawthrone	Standish O'Grady	Young E. Allison
Nicolo Machiavelli	Stanley Weyman	Zane Grey
O. F. Walton	Stella Benson	
Oscar Wilde	Stella M. Francis	

www.ingramcontent.com/pod-product-compliance
Lightning Source LLC
Chambersburg PA
CBHW030141200626
46812CB00015B/518